GET OUTSiDE GUIDE

All Things Adventure, Exploration, and Fun!

By Nancy Honovich and Julie Beer

Foreword by Richard Louv, author of *Last Child in the Woods*

WASHINGTON, D.C.

CONTENTS

Nature Around Town

Let's Go to the Park

Getting OUTSIDE

THESE DAYS, with technological advances at an all-time high, it's easy to miss what's happening outdoors. We can become so absorbed in the screens before our faces that we forget just how fascinating and amazing the world around us really is.

Not only can nature help reduce your stress, it can also help make you healthier and even smarter and more creative. Some of the most fun you can have is right outside, whether you're hiking a mountain trail or stargazing in your own backyard. Getting outside gets you into real-life adventures. You can create awesome sand castles at the beach, find the hidden life in a creek, spot wildlife in the woods, or build a birdbath in your very own yard.

Get Outside Guide will lead you through the outdoors near and far, from exploring forests and climbing rocks to finding nature even in the city! Whether you live in the country or in an urban metropolis, this book will reveal the wonders of nature right at your doorstep. With activities, ideas, and projects to help you explore, you'll be ready to create your own wilderness adventures. So let's get outside—where you'll discover games to play, animals to meet, and places to explore!

—Richard Louv

HOW TO USE This Book

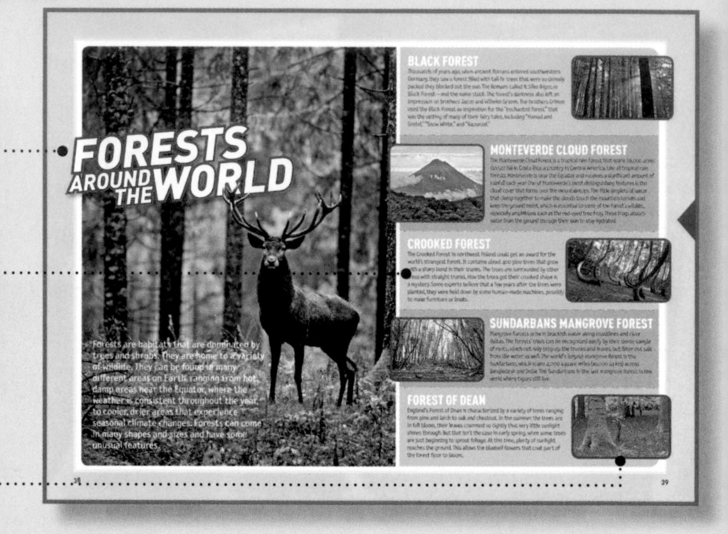

FORESTS AROUND THE WORLD

Forests are habitats that are dominated by trees and shrubs. They are home to a variety of wildlife. They can be found in many different areas on Earth, ranging from hot, damp areas near the Equator, where the weather is consistent throughout the year, to cooler, drier areas that experience seasonal climate changes. Forests can come in many shapes and sizes and have some unusual features.

BLACK FOREST

MONTEVERDE CLOUD FOREST

CROOKED FOREST

SUNDARBANS MANGROVE FOREST

FOREST OF DEAN

38

39

The title tells you what kind of areas or environments will be featured in a particular section.

On each of these spreads you will be introduced to five places around the world that are specifically connected to the habitat or area that is being discussed in the section.

Pictures of each of these places will give you an idea of what they look like.

RAIN FORESTS

Rain forests are located in areas that receive more than 70 inches (178 cm) of rainfall each year. There are two types of rain forests: temperate and tropical.

Temperate rain forests occur in coastal areas between the tropical and polar regions. Tongass National Forest in Alaska is the world's largest temperate rain forest.

Tropical rain forests grow near the Equator, in areas such as South and Central America, West Africa, and Southeast Asia. The world's largest is the Amazon Rain Forest in South America. It covers as much land as the 48 contiguous U.S. states!

56

EXPLORE

LISTEN UP

In a rain forest, the upper parts of trees grow closely together and form the forest's ceiling, or canopy. These leafy surroundings can make it difficult for the birds and monkeys that live there to see each other, so they must rely on verbal communication to get by. If you're in a rain forest, close your eyes and tune in. Can you hear any howls, whistles, or shrills?

LOOK DOWN

Life in a rain forest isn't just challenging for the animals; plants in a densely packed canopy must also come up with clever ways to obtain the resources they need to survive. The strangler fig tree, found in tropical rain forests, grows from seeds that have been dispersed on high branches of trees. The seeds shoot roots down to the forest floor. These roots slowly "strangle" the older tree from which they grow by soaking up most of the water and nutrients from the ground.

ANIMALS

Animal life isn't limited to just the canopies of temperate and tropical rain forests. Birds, such as macaws and bald eagles, can be found above the canopy, in treetops that reach 130 feet (40 m) above the ground. Big cats, such as jaguars and clouded leopards, dwell in the understory, an area just below the canopy. Meanwhile, the forest floor is home to insects, mammals, and amphibians.

HAVE FUN

Grab a camera and snap photos of some of the unusual sights you see. Experiment with camera angles by getting down on your stomach or climbing a tree and shooting downward. You may also want to experiment with natural light. Sunlight shining through a dense canopy can speckle the trees with uneven light, so you may find that the best time to take photos is when the skies are cloudy. After you're done, you can share your favorite pictures with the world by uploading them to NG Kids My Shot at kids-myshot.nationalgeographic.com.

fun fact

Giant rodents called capybaras live in the Amazon rain forest. The rodents stand up to 25 inches (64 cm) at the shoulders. That's about as tall as some German shepherds!

57

The "Have Fun" section gives you ideas for outdoor games that inspire exploration and adventure.

The "Animals" section highlights some popular creatures that you may find in the area or environment that you are reading about.

The first two text blocks on each of these spreads discuss plants, animals, or other parts of nature that you have to listen for or look for.

Introductory text gives you an overview of the particular habitat or area you will be reading about on the following page.

Seasons vary around the globe, and this text gives you an overview of how an environment might change as the seasons change.

Text blocks for each season highlight something special or unique that happens at a particular place during a particular season.

Pictures of landscapes or animals in their habitats in a particular season give you an idea of what different places look like when the seasons change.

WATER in all seasons

At any time of year, you can find wildlife in a body of water, though the animals you see in one season may be different from those you see in another. Some animals temporarily leave home because colder climates make it hard for them to find food. Others migrate seasonally to mate and have babies. Discover the underwater habitats that some animals call home in spring, summer, fall, and winter.

SPRING

In early spring in tropical areas such as the Caribbean, the first adult leatherback sea turtles (*Dermochelys coriacea*) can be spotted returning to the same beaches where they hatched. Once they arrive, the turtles wait until nightfall to dig a hole in the sand in which they lay their own eggs. The turtles then return to the sea. When the hatchlings emerge from the eggs—up to 75 days later—they, too, head to the sea.

FALL

By fall, many freshwater rivers and streams are filled with sockeye salmon (*Oncorhynchus nerka*) that have migrated from the Pacific Ocean to spawn or lay their eggs. These freshwater environments are the same places where the adult salmon hatched years earlier. The salmon's journey "home" is a dangerous one. They must swim upstream against currents and dodge potential predators such as bears. These salmon can be found as far away as the Canadian Arctic, Japan, and Siberia.

SUMMER

Although they look like autumn leaves, cownose rays (*Rhinoptera bonasus*) are a sign of summer in the northeastern Atlantic coast. They travel in large groups—sometimes as many as 10,000! These rays swim from Brazil to the Chesapeake Bay in Maryland, U.S.A., to give birth to pups. They can be found in the Atlantic Ocean from New England to the Caribbean and Mexico all the way to northern South America and western Africa.

WINTER

Many animals try to escape cold winter temperatures by migrating to warmer climates, but North American beavers (*Castor canadensis*) remain in their pond environment year-round. Their secret lies in the lodges they create from tree branches, mud, and stones. The lodges shelter them from the winter chill and protect them from possible predators. To feed, the furry rodents dive through an underwater entryway and access their winter food supply—the branches of trees and shrubs.

22 23

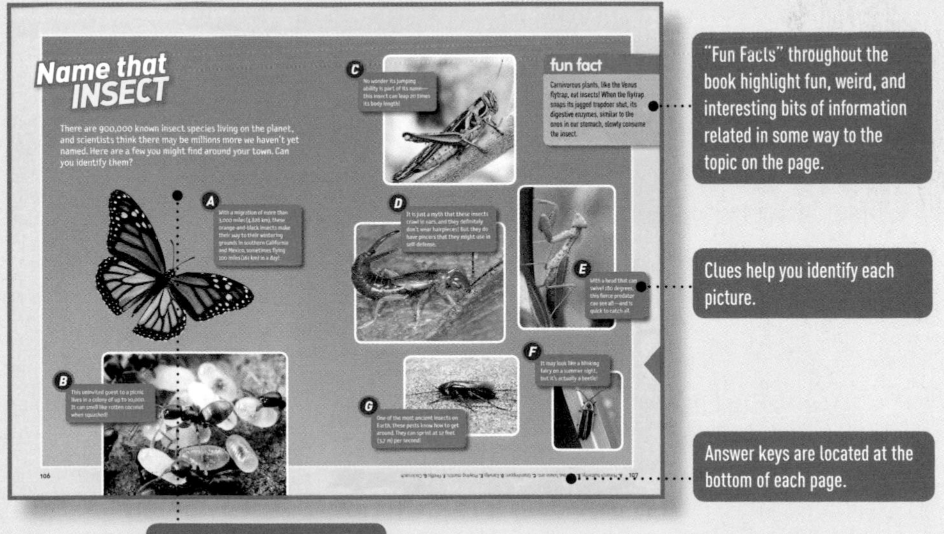

Name that INSECT

There are 900,000 known insect species living on the planet, and scientists think there may be millions more we haven't yet named. Here are a few you might find around your town. Can you identify them?

A With a migration of more than 3,000 miles (4,828 km), these orange-and-black insects make their way to their wintering grounds in southern California and Mexico, sometimes flying 100 miles (161 km) in a day!

B This uninvited guest to a picnic lives in a colony of up to 10,000. It can smell like rotten coconut when squashed!

C No wonder its jumping ability is part of its name—this insect can leap 20 times its body length!

D It is just a myth that these insects crawl in ears, and they definitely don't wear hairpieces! But they do have pincers that they might use in self-defense.

E With a head that can swivel 180 degrees, this fierce predator can see all—and is quick to catch all.

F It may look like a blinking fairy on a summer night, but it's actually a beetle!

G One of the most ancient insects on Earth, these pests know how to get around. They can sprint at 12 feet (3.7 m) per second!

fun fact

Carnivorous plants, like the Venus flytrap, eat insects! When the flytrap snaps its jagged trapdoor shut, its digestive enzymes, similar to the ones in our stomach, slowly consume the insect.

106 107

"Fun Facts" throughout the book highlight fun, weird, and interesting bits of information related in some way to the topic on the page.

Clues help you identify each picture.

Answer keys are located at the bottom of each page.

These "ID" spreads challenge you to name different animals, flowers, trees, clouds, and even outdoor sports.

HABiTATS AROUND THE WORLD

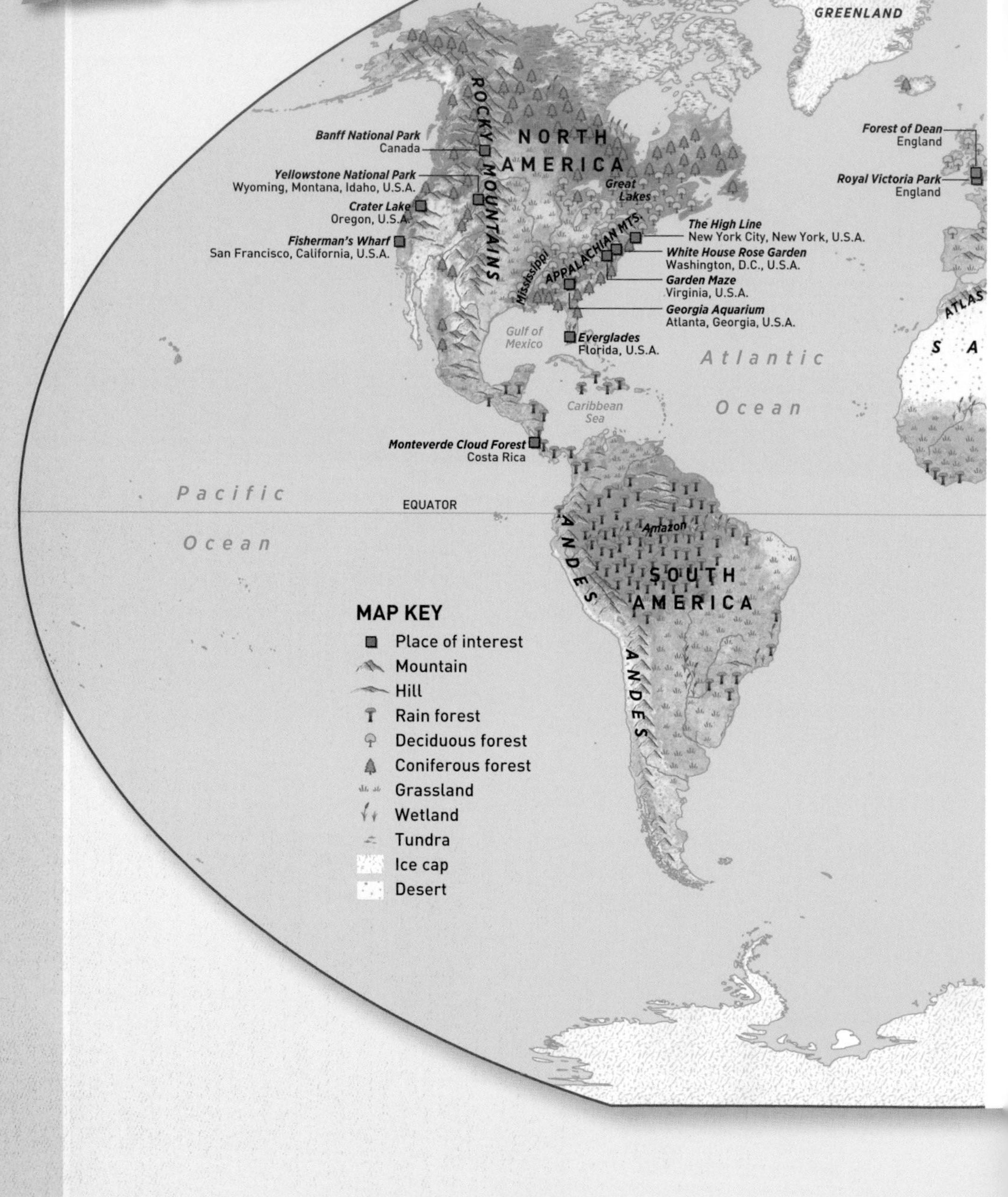

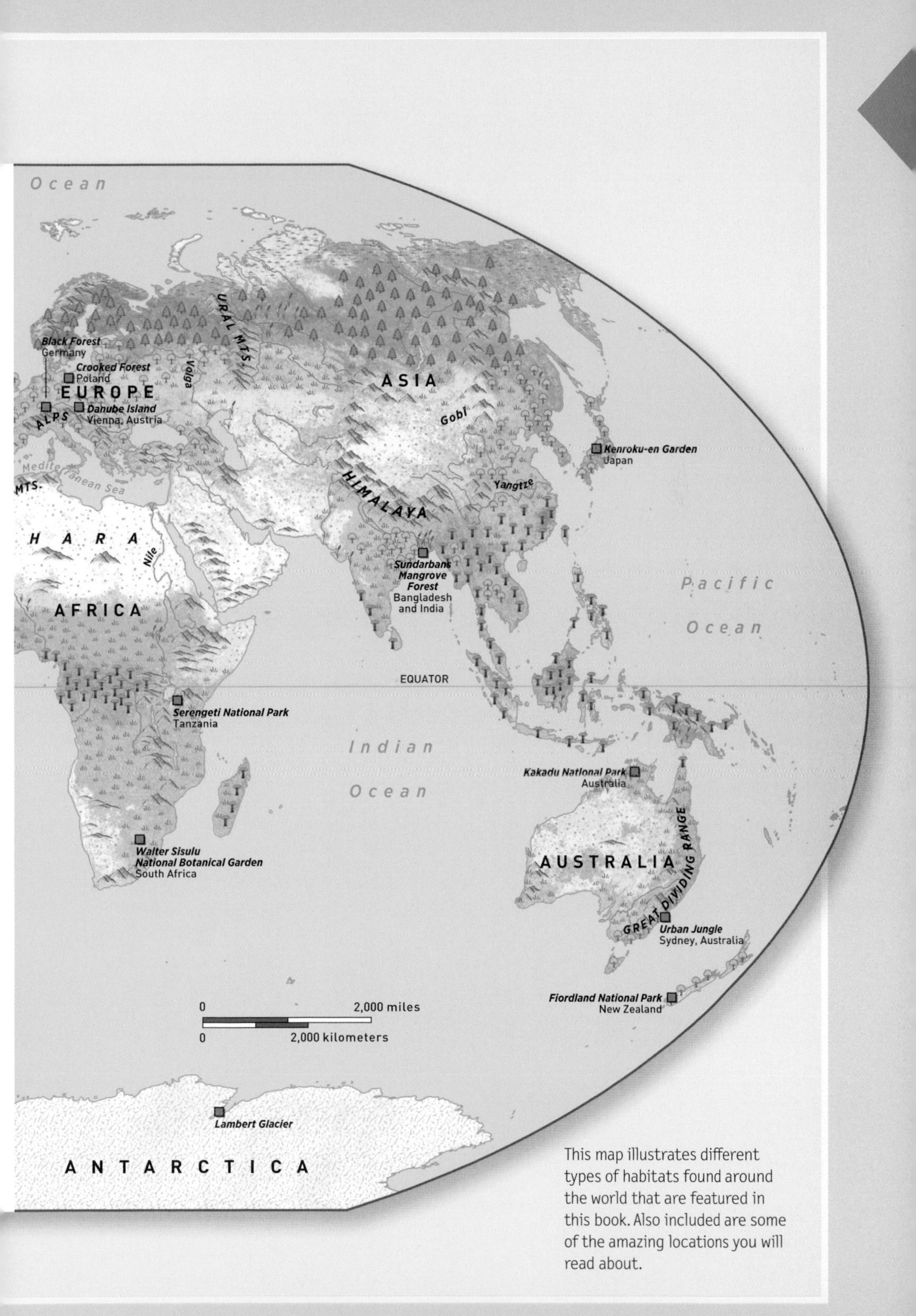

This map illustrates different types of habitats found around the world that are featured in this book. Also included are some of the amazing locations you will read about.

LET'S GET
WET!

WATER EVERYWHERE

More than 70 percent of Earth's surface is covered with water. Although oceans make up most of that percentage, water is also found in rivers, streams, ponds, and lakes. It exists in the atmosphere as a gas called water vapor. Only about 2.5 percent of Earth's water is fresh and less than 1 percent of that is accessible to humans. Read on to discover five amazing bodies of water.

PACIFIC OCEAN

There are four oceans in the world, all of which are interconnected. They include the Arctic, Atlantic, Indian, and Pacific. The world's largest and deepest is the Pacific Ocean. It spans nearly half the globe, covering 70 million square miles (180 sq km). Its deepest point, the Mariana Trench, descends 35,840 feet (10,924 m). That's so deep that if Mount Everest, the world's tallest mountain, was dropped there it would completely disappear!

YANGTZE RIVER

All rivers have a starting point or source. This source can be a melting glacier, a lake, or even a spring. The Yangtze River—the longest river in Asia at 3,988 miles (6,418 km) long—has its source in the Kunlun Mountains of southwestern China. The river flows from this source for about 3,720 miles (5,987 km) and empties into the South China Sea. That's farther than Washington, D.C., to California! But the Yangtze River isn't the world's longest river. That distinction goes to the Nile in eastern Africa. It's 4,132 miles (6,650 km) long!

CRATER LAKE

Lakes and ponds are often created when water collects in a shallow basin, or hole, in the earth. The basin is typically the result of a natural force, such as erosion, or in the case of Oregon's Crater Lake, a volcanic explosion. In 5700 B.C., a now dormant volcano called Mount Mazama erupted. The eruption expelled so much pumice and ash from the volcano that its summit collapsed and formed a large crater known as a caldera. Eventually, snowmelt collected in the caldera and formed a lake more than 1,900 feet (579 m) deep.

LAMBERT GLACIER

More than 68 percent of Earth's freshwater supply can be found in glaciers and ice caps. Glaciers are large sheets of ice that flow over the ground in cold places. They form when layers of snow build up over many years. As new snow piles up, it pushes down on older snow, turning it into ice. The Lambert Glacier, located in east Antarctica, is about 60 miles (400 km) long and 8,202 feet (2,500 m) deep. It is one of the largest glaciers in the world!

EVERGLADES

The Everglades is a region of wetlands in southern Florida that is formed partly by a moving body of water. During the wet season, from June to November, rainwater causes the Kissimmee River to surge south into Lake Okeechobee. The water spills over the banks of the lake and floods low-lying areas of saw grass. The shallow river continues south. It fills marshes that flow around islands and flow into coastal mangrove forests. Eventually the river empties into Florida Bay. In the late 1940s, a series of levees, canals, and pumping stations were built to clear the land for agricultural and urban development. These structures diverted much of the water flowing directly from Lake Okeechobee.

AT THE BEACH

Beaches are narrow strips of land—made up of sediments—that lie along the edge of an ocean, lake, or river. Beaches form when water and wind beat against land over thousands of years. This continual action loosens rocks from the land or breaks the land down into tiny particles. The wind and water then carry these sediments to the shore, where they deposit them. Over time, the sediments build up and form a beach.

EXPLORE

LOOK DOWN

Is the sand on your beach brown or white? If so, it may be composed of quartz, a mineral that makes up landmasses. Quartz is the most common mineral in sand, but it's not the only one. You can identify the different minerals by their colors. Red grains are usually garnet and green grains are olivine. Pink sand, which is common in the tropics, comes from weathered coral, while black sand is the result of hardened lava from volcanoes.

LOOK AROUND

How many seashells can you see? Chances are a lot! Seashells can be found scattered across most beaches. The shells, which come in many colors, shapes, and sizes, are the protective coverings of mollusks—a group of animals without a backbone that live in the water or in damp areas. Mollusks can include sea slugs, oval-shaped marine animals called chitons, mussels, clams, and deep-sea creatures called tusk shells. Mollusks have soft bodies, so they rely on their tough shells to protect themselves from predators and rough ocean waves.

ANIMALS

Mollusks aren't the only animals that live at the beach. Birds, such as pelicans and seagulls, and crustaceans, such as crabs, lobsters, and shrimp, make their home at the beach. In addition, the ocean is home to many varieties of fish.

HAVE FUN

Did you know that you can use the shape of a seashell to identify the mollusk that it housed? Collect as many different seashells as possible. Then examine the shapes. Long, flat shells with eight overlapping plates are typical of chitons. Tube-shaped shells that are open on both ends belong to tusk shells. Hinged shells are made by bivalves, such as clams, oysters, and mussels. Large spiral shells are the work of gastropods, such as conches, sea slugs, and cowries.

fun fact

If a sea star loses its arm, a new one grows back in its place.

Build a SAND CASTLE

SUPPLY LIST

- Big shovel for heavy sand lifting; small shovel (a garden trowel will work) for detail work
- A large bucket for hauling water; one or two smaller buckets (or fun-shaped containers) for forming towers
- Measuring spoons or scoopers for interesting designs; sticks for writing
- Bits of nature, such as seashells, feathers, and seaweed for decorations

WHEN YOU FIND YOURSELF AT THE BEACH,
building a sand castle is practically a requirement.
Here's how to build a fortress that will stand above the others.

fun fact

It has been estimated that there are seven quintillion, five hundred quadrillion grains of sand on Earth!

STEPS

1. Sketch out your floor plan with a shovel so all the builders involved can envision the construction site—and know where NOT to step.
2. Start bringing sand in on top of the floor plan and build up. Remember: You'll need this sand to be quite moist.
3. Pack down the side walls with your shovel or hands. This keeps the structure solid and will keep the waves out!
4. Dig a trench around the perimeter to serve as your moat. This gives your castle a distinct look, and it serves as extra protection against waves!
5. Fill up the smaller buckets with wet sand and pack them right to the rim. Flip them over to build towers.
6. Decorate! Carve windows in the side of towers using your measuring scoops, press seashells into the walls, and add a feather to the tallest tower to act as a flag.

Time: 30 minutes or longer

WHAT IS SAND?

Sand is tiny pieces of worn-down rock. It usually starts out as gravel and gets worn by rain or wind, or whittled down in a river as it is tossed along downstream. Eventually it gets picked up in the wind or moved by water or ice and ends up in the ocean as sediment.

Name that SHELL

Seashells are like scattered treasures waiting to be discovered. Can you identify what kind these are? The next time you're at the ocean, see if you can recognize some! Don't forget to look for signs at your beach to confirm that shell collecting is allowed. If you live closer to a lake or pond you may also find shells on their shores. Go find out!

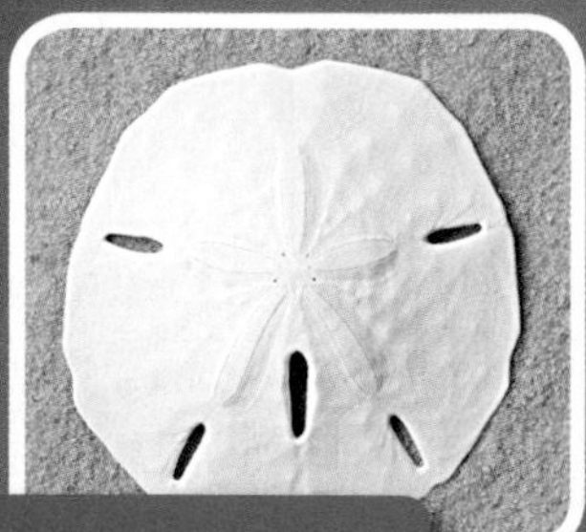

A With a distinct five-pointed sea star shape on its back, this seashell is valuable just by its name!

B When they're alive, these creatures can be found on the rocky shore, clinging to rocks with tiny little fibers. Once they've washed ashore, they are smooth and deep purple.

C

Before it found its way to the beach, this shell, which can reach two feet (60 cm) in length, was home to the largest snail in North America.

D

Used as money and jewelry for hundreds of years, these smooth shells are small enough to scoop up several in your hand at once.

fun fact

The oldest living creature ever recorded was a quahog clam found off the coast of Iceland. It was believed to be more than 405 years old!

E

Mary, Mary Quite Contrary might be able to help you identify this shell. This saltwater clam can be found on beaches around the world.

F

You might feel like you're being watched when you spot this shell. A dark spot in the middle has led some to call this a shark's eye—but its more common name doesn't come from the sea, but rather from something overhead.

G

When it's clinging to a rock, you can't see the prize that's inside, but when washed up on a beach, its rainbow interior sparkles.

A. Sand dollar; **B.** Mussels; **C.** Florida horse conch; **D.** Cowrie; **E.** Cockleshell; **F.** Moon shell; **G.** Abalone

WATER in all seasons

SPRING

In early spring in tropical areas such as the Caribbean, the first adult leatherback sea turtles *(Dermochelys coriacea)* can be spotted returning to the same beaches where they hatched. Once they arrive, the turtles wait until nightfall to dig a hole in the sand in which they lay their own eggs. The turtles then return to the sea. When the hatchlings emerge from the eggs—up to 75 days later—they, too, head to the sea.

SUMMER

Although they look like autumn leaves, cownose rays *(Rhinoptera bonasus)* are a sign of summer in the northeastern Atlantic coast. They travel in large groups—sometimes as many as 10,000! These rays swim from Brazil to the Chesapeake Bay in Maryland, U.S.A., to give birth to pups. They can be found in the Atlantic Ocean from New England to the Caribbean and Mexico all the way to northern South America and western Africa.

At any time of year, you can find wildlife in a body of water, though the animals you see in one season may be different from those you see in another. Some animals temporarily leave home because colder climates make it hard for them to find food. Others migrate seasonally to mate and have babies. Discover the underwater habitats that some animals call home in spring, summer, fall, and winter.

FALL

By fall, many freshwater rivers and streams are filled with sockeye salmon *(Oncorhynchus nerka)* that have migrated from the Pacific Ocean to spawn or lay their eggs. These freshwater environments are the same places where the adult salmon hatched years earlier. The salmon's journey "home" is a dangerous one. They must swim upstream against currents and dodge potential predators such as bears. These salmon can be found as far away as the Canadian Arctic, Japan, and Siberia.

WINTER

Many animals try to escape cold winter temperatures by migrating to warmer climates, but North American beavers *(Castor canadensis)* remain in their pond environment year-round. Their secret lies in the lodges they create from tree branches, mud, and stones. The lodges shelter them from the winter chill and protect them from possible predators. To feed, the furry rodents dive through an underwater entryway and access their winter food supply—the branches of trees and shrubs.

RiVERS & STREAMS

Rivers often begin flowing from their sources as smaller bodies of water called creeks. As the creeks travel, they grow into streams. The streams flow from a higher altitude to a lower one increasing in speed along the way. Then the water usually merges with other streams to create a river. Rivers eventually empty into another body of water. This could be another river, a lake, or an ocean. Now that you know the basics about rivers and streams you're ready to explore further!

EXPLORE

LOOK DOWN

As you walk along the banks of a river or stream, you may notice that it starts to curve. This is called a meander. Meanders are formed when the moving water erodes the outer banks of the river or stream. The water carries the eroded sediment downstream and deposits it on the inner banks. It takes many years for a meander to form.

LOOK AROUND

There are many different types of plants that grow by rivers and streams. Some plants, such as water reeds, grow along the shore. Others, such as the lotus flower, are rooted in the soil or sediment at the bottom of the water and grow their leaves or flowers on the water's surface. What kinds of plants do you see around the rivers and streams where you live?

ANIMALS

Many animals also live in or near rivers and streams. For example, in the Mississippi River, you'll find fish such as sturgeon, paddlefish, and spotted bass; birds such as the Great Egret; reptiles such as the American alligator; and mammals such as the North American river otter. What kinds of animals live in or near the rivers and streams near you?

HAVE FUN

Visit a local park or recreation area that has a river you can explore. Bring a blank notebook and some colored pencils with you. Then take a ride in a canoe, rowboat, or paddleboat or just walk along the riverbank. Look out for different plants and animals along the way and draw pictures of what you see. You may also want to take notes about what you see, hear, and feel during your trip. Keep your notebook as a nature journal and add to it whenever you have an outdoor adventure!

fun fact

During the wet season (December to June), the Amazon River can grow from 2.5 miles (4 km) to 31 miles (50 km) wide!

Name that TiDE POOL ANiMAL

When the tide goes out in rocky, coastal areas, some water gets left behind in pools and crevices. These spots are called tide pools and many different creatures like to hang out in them. See if you can name the tide pool animals on these pages.

A

This creature is always on the lookout for a new home. Snail shells are usually its preference, but with five pairs of legs, you can't call it a slow poke!

B

Nemo and his father lived inside one of these. When their tentacles are open they are ready for food; when they're folded in, they're likely munching.

C

These drifters don't have much say where they end up, but often they show up in tide pools. They may be soft and squishy, but their tentacles are stunning.

D

The webbing between this animal's short, triangular arms is a clue to its name. Sensors on the end of each of its arms can sense light and detect prey.

E

After grazing on algae, this tide pool creature finds the perfect parking spot on a rock and hunkers down, sealing water underneath itself to keep its body moist during low tide.

F

Call it a tide pool salad. This leafy green creature can get dry and stiff at low tide, but it bounces right back once the water comes in.

fun fact

A tide pool is one tough neighborhood! When the tide is in, waves come crashing; when the tide is out, animals are exposed to sun, cold weather, and even fresh water from rain. When you look closely at tide pool creatures you'll find they all have adaptations to survive these harsh conditions.

A. Hermit crab; **B.** Sea anemone; **C.** Jellyfish; **D.** Bat star; **E.** Limpet; **F.** Sea lettuce

Make a PAPER BOAT (THAT FLOATS!)

EXPLORE A CREEK OR STREAM BY SETTING SAIL!

With nothing more than some paper and a few folding tricks you can make your very own vessel to investigate the waters' currents.

fun fact

There are three million ships on the ocean floor. Scientists are finding that some have created an artificial habitat for marine life.

SUPPLY LIST

- Paper
- Sticky tape

STEPS

1. Take a piece of plain—or colorful—paper and place it in front of you with the shorter side at the top. Fold the paper in half from top to bottom.
2. Fold left to right to find the center, and reopen. Bring the top two corners together to the middle, forming a point, and crease.
3. Fold the top flap at the bottom of the paper up; turn over and fold the other flap up. Fold the triangle tabs in over each other so you have a triangle.
4. Pop open the center like a hat, push the pointed sides to meet, and crease down so that you now have a square.
5. With the opening facing you, fold the top layer up to meet the other point. Turn the paper over and repeat.
6. Gently pull apart the top two points while pushing out with your fingers to form the bottom of the boat.
7. Reinforce corners with clear tape and also tape around the bottom to keep your boat dry. Now you are ready to launch your craft!

Time: about 10 minutes

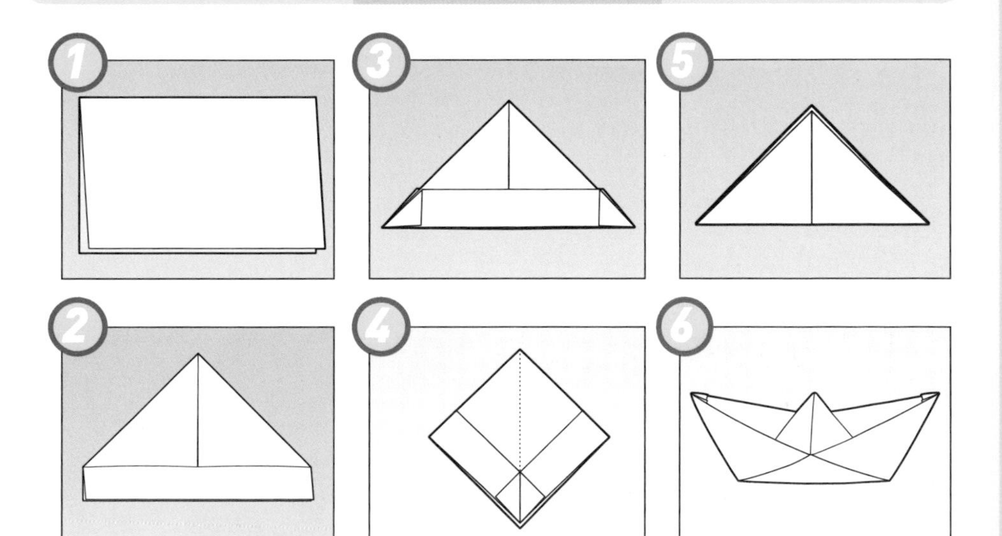

LAKES & PONDS

Lakes and ponds, which are bodies of water surrounded by land, are formed when a basin in the earth fills with water. Most basins were created by the movement of glaciers, but some are man-made or are the result of volcanic activity or a meteorite strike. During the Ice Age, glaciers leveled mountains and carved out depressions such as valleys as they moved. Eventually, the climate warmed and the glaciers began to melt and fill the depressions with water. How many lakes and ponds are in your town?

EXPLORE

LOOK DOWN

On a warm summer day, dip your legs into a lake or pond until you are standing knee-deep in the water. The water should feel cooler at the bottom and warmer near the surface. Why? In the summer, warm air temperature and the sun's rays heat the water near the surface. Since warm water is less dense, or lighter, than cold water, it remains on top. As the air temperature begins to dip in the fall, so does the water temperature at the surface. The water cools until it eventually freezes in the winter. The frozen water remains at the top because ice is less dense than water.

ANIMALS

In the spring and summer, ponds and lakes are buzzing with activity. You might see a dragonfly nymph crawling up the stalk of a plant, a water strider skating, or a pond turtle navigating through grass. In addition, ponds and lakes are home to many fish. But what happens to the animals when these bodies of water freeze in the winter? Some animals burrow or migrate to escape. Others simply swim to the bottom of the pond or lake, where waters are warmer thanks to the insulating layer of ice above.

LOOK AROUND

Check out the color of a pond in your town. It's most likely green. The color is the result of algae, plant-like organisms that lack stems, roots, and leaves. Like plants, algae contain a green pigment called chlorophyll, which gives them their color, and thus makes the water look green. Algae feed on phosphorus and nitrogen, so when these two elements are abundant in the water, the algae begin to bloom, making the pond look even greener. The excess algae look like a slimy coating. You probably know it as pond scum.

HAVE FUN

Skipping rocks is a great game to play when at a pond or lake. Find a rock that is skinny, flat, and round. Hold your rock in a way that's comfortable. Stand along the shore of the lake or pond with your feet shoulder-width apart facing sideways to the water. If you are right-handed, you should stand so your left hand is closest to the water. Do the opposite if you are left-handed. When you're ready, flick your rock across the water, swiftly twisting your wrist as you toss. See how many times your rock skips above the surface!

fun fact

Some lakes contain salt and minerals, which come from dissolved rocks. The Dead Sea in Israel is one of the saltiest lakes in the world. Since salt water in the Dead Sea is very dense, people can float in it.

Make an UNDERWATER SCOPE

WHAT BETTER WAY TO CHECK OUT A CREEK OR STREAM than to see what's happening inside it. Spy on what's going on underwater with your own underwater scope.

fun fact

The leaves of a Victoria giant water lily, which is native to South America, can be as wide as 9.8 feet (3 m)!

SUPPLY LIST

- Empty coffee can
- Plastic wrap
- Rubber band
- Colored construction paper
- Glue
- Scissors

STEPS

1. Using a can opener, cut the end off of an empty coffee can so both ends are open.
2. If you want to add color to your can, cut a piece of construction paper to fit the size of the coffee can all the way around. Then glue it on.
3. Cut a large piece of plastic wrap and cover one end of the can. Secure the plastic wrap with a heavy-duty rubber band. Place the scope in the water with the plastic wrap side facing down and take a look at whatever decides to swim by!
4. If you want to make a scope for deeper water, follow the same steps but use a longer piece of PVC pipe in place of the coffee can.

Time: about 15 minutes

HOW DO WATER STRIDERS FLOAT?

How do water striders—those insects that zoom across the surface of ponds—stay afloat? Scientists figured out their legs are covered in tiny hairs, each of which have little grooves in them that trap air. All of this increases the insects' water resistance and keeps them afloat.

Name that SEA ANiMAL

Animals can be found everywhere at the beach—in or out of the water and sometimes in between. Can you name these common, close-to-shore sea animals?

A

These cuddly, furry creatures swim close to shore along the Pacific Ocean, where they like to dive for mussels and then crack them open using a rock.

B

This slow-moving gentle giant is also known as a sea cow, but it never leaves the water. It munches on vegetation in coastal waters—and sometimes even meanders up rivers.

C

A few lengths of a swimming pool away from the beach, these fierce-looking, but generally nonthreatening, creatures are combing the ocean floor looking for food. Hint: Take one look at its face and you've hit the nail on the head.

D

Often found in shallow waters and not afraid of snorkelers, these creatures are flat like a pancake and smooth as silk.

fun fact

Early explorers to the New World mistook manatees for mermaids! In 1493, Columbus reported seeing three mermaids—who were later assumed to be manatees—playing in Caribbean waters.

E

This reptilian wonder can grow to be as big as 8.5 feet (2.6 m) long and migrates thousands of miles every year. Unlike some of its relatives, its shell isn't hard—it's flexible like your dress-up shoes (hint, hint).

G

With a pouch like that, who needs a fishing net? These creatures are found scooping up fish along coastlines and sitting on docks of the bay.

F

These friendly mammals frequent harbors and bays. When they come up for air, they make a noise that sounds like a sneeze!

A. Sea otter; **B.** Manatee; **C.** Hammerhead shark; **D.** Stingray; **E.** Leatherback turtle; **F.** Harbor porpoise; **G.** Pelican

JOURNEY
THROUGH THE
TREES

FORESTS AROUND THE WORLD

Forests are habitats that are dominated by trees and shrubs. They are home to a variety of wildlife. They can be found in many different areas on Earth, ranging from hot, damp areas near the Equator, where the weather is consistent throughout the year, to cooler, drier areas that experience seasonal climate changes. Forests can come in many shapes and sizes and have some unusual features.

BLACK FOREST

Thousands of years ago, when ancient Romans entered southwestern Germany, they saw a forest filled with tall fir trees that were so densely packed they blocked out the sun. The Romans called it *Silva Nigra*, or Black Forest—and the name stuck. The forest's darkness also left an impression on brothers Jacob and Wilhelm Grimm. The brothers Grimm used the Black Forest as inspiration for the "enchanted forest" that was the setting of many of their fairy tales, including "Hansel and Gretel," "Snow White," and "Rapunzel."

MONTEVERDE CLOUD FOREST

The Monteverde Cloud Forest is a tropical rain forest that spans 26,000 acres (10,522 ha) in Costa Rica, a country in Central America. Like all tropical rain forests, Monteverde is near the Equator and receives a significant amount of rainfall each year. One of Monteverde's most distinguishing features is the cloud cover that forms over the mountaintops. The little droplets of water that clump together to make the clouds touch the mountain terrain and keep the ground moist, which is essential to some of the forest's wildlife, especially amphibians such as the red-eyed tree frog. These frogs absorb water from the ground through their skin to stay hydrated.

CROOKED FOREST

The Crooked Forest in northwest Poland could get an award for the world's strangest forest. It contains about 400 pine trees that grow with a sharp bend in their trunks. The trees are surrounded by other trees with straight trunks. How the trees got their crooked shape is a mystery. Some experts believe that a few years after the trees were planted, they were held down by some human-made machines, possibly to make furniture or boats.

SUNDARBANS MANGROVE FOREST

Mangrove forests grow in brackish water along coastlines and river deltas. The forests' trees can be recognized easily by their dense tangle of roots, which not only prop up the trunks and leaves, but filter out salt from the water as well. The world's largest mangrove forest is the Sundarbans, which spans 4,000 square miles (10,000 sq km) across Bangladesh and India. The Sundarbans is the last mangrove forest in the world where tigers still live.

FOREST OF DEAN

England's Forest of Dean is characterized by a variety of trees ranging from pine and larch to oak and chestnut. In the summer, the trees are in full bloom, their leaves crammed so tightly that very little sunlight shines through. But that isn't the case in early spring, when some trees are just beginning to sprout foliage. At this time, plenty of sunlight reaches the ground. This allows the bluebell flowers that coat part of the forest floor to bloom.

CONiFEROUS FORESTS

Coniferous forests are usually found in the Northern Hemisphere in large parts of northern North America and across northern Europe, Russia, and Asia. These areas have long winters, short summers, and plenty of rainfall. The forests are populated with trees such as spruces, pines, and firs, which produce cones and have thin, needle-like leaves. Most of these trees have soft, flexible branches that point downward—an adaptation that allows snow to slide off.

EXPLORE

LOOK UP

Redwood trees are the tallest in the world. One tree, nicknamed "Hyperion," measured more than 379 feet (115 m) in 2011. That's taller than the Statue of Liberty! Why do these trees grow so tall? Like all green plants, redwoods need sunlight for photosynthesis, a process they use to make food. But getting light isn't easy in a forest that's crowded with other trees. A redwood must outgrow its competition to get the most sunlight possible. How tall are the trees where you live?

LOOK DOWN

The forest floor is home to many different species of insects. Discover what insects are lurking in your forest by conducting an investigation. Look for insects in fallen logs, on the leaves of plants, on the surface of the soil, and along creeks. Draw a picturc of an insect you spotted and jot down any interesting physical characteristics and behaviors in a notebook.

ANIMALS

To see wildlife, your best bet is to explore the forest during the spring and summer. In the winter, when food isn't plentiful, many of the forest's animals hibernate or migrate to different regions. Next time you're in the woods, see if you can spot black bears, moose or elk, owls, bald eagles, and wolves.

HAVE FUN

Challenge your friends to a game of "Rock, Tree, Bridge." You'll need at least six players. First break up into two teams. Determine a starting line and a finish line. Have the teams line up at the starting line. When someone yells, "Go!" the first person on each team crouches down and pretends to be a rock. The second person in line hops over the "rock" and stands up with his arms raised, pretending to be a tree. The third person in line runs around the "tree" once and then scoots down to the ground and arches her body in a bridge position. The first person then crawls under the "bridge" and crouches down to form a "rock" again. Each team repeats this pattern until reaching the finish line.

fun fact

One of the largest pinecones in the world is the Coulter pine. It can grow up to 16 inches (41 cm) long and weigh up to 10 pounds (4.5 kg)!

GAIN A GREATER APPRECIATION FOR ALL THE WORK spiders put into their webs by making your very own!

fun fact

A spider's web may look delicate, but it's strong! Spider silk is five times as strong as steel of the same diameter.

SUPPLY LIST

- Yarn or string
- A notebook and pencil

STEPS

1. Before you do anything, go on a hunt for spiderwebs. Spiders spin all kinds of designs. Spend some time studying one and sketch out the design in a notebook. Webs can be found everywhere, from crevices of trees to in between grasses to inside shrubs. Look high and low!
2. Next, start spinning your web. There's no limit to the size—just find two trees and start unwinding your "silk" (your yarn or string). Try to copy the pattern you sketched.
3. Compare your web to the spider's web. Try making a large web and a tiny one.

Time: about 25 minutes

HOW DO SPIDERS AVOID GETTING TANGLED?

Spiderwebs are sticky business, so how come spiders don't get caught in their own webs? It turns out that a spider's web isn't all sticky—the spiral parts are generally sticky, the spokes are not. But spiders do have to touch the sticky parts while building the web. To get around that, their legs have tiny hairs that prevent them from getting stuck. Spiders also have an oily substance on them that repels the sticky stuff.

Name that LEAF

Telling one kind of tree from another can be tricky, but their leaves are unique enough to give you a clue as to what species they belong to. Can you identify the trees that match these leaves? Go outside and observe the kinds of trees and leaves where you live.

A

These trees grow a certain nut that is a popular wintertime snack. It's found in hard, oval-shaped shells.

B

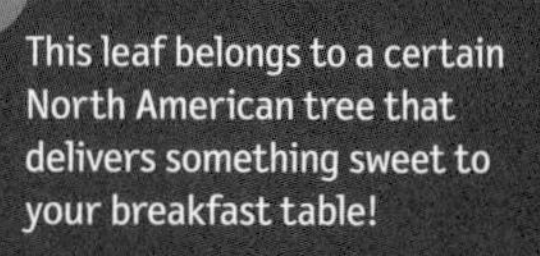

This leaf belongs to a certain North American tree that delivers something sweet to your breakfast table!

C

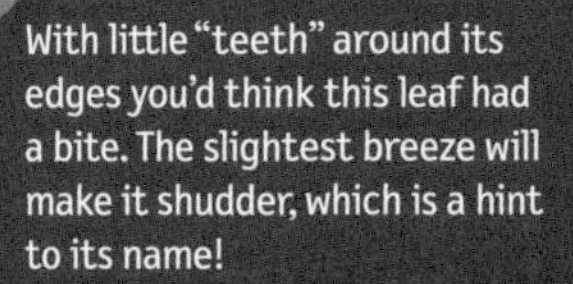

With little "teeth" around its edges you'd think this leaf had a bite. The slightest breeze will make it shudder, which is a hint to its name!

D

These thin needles come from trees that also grow brown cones.

E

Leaves from these types of trees look similar to fans. They are found in tropical areas around the world.

F

As a general rule, these leaves grow in clusters of three. Just remember: You can look, but don't touch. This leaf will likely leave you itching!

G

Dark green leaves with bright red berries are the perfect color combination for this tree used for holiday decorating.

fun fact

The average maple tree drops 600,000 leaves every fall.

A. Sweet chestnut; **B.** Maple; **C.** Quaking aspen; **D.** Pine; **E.** Palm tree; **F.** Poison oak; **G.** American holly

DECiDUOUS FORESTS

Deciduous forests are found in areas of the world with moist summers and cold winters, where temperatures dip below freezing. These areas mainly include the northeastern United States, Canada, and parts of Europe and Asia. Although trees with color-changing leaves dominate deciduous forests, they aren't the forests' only plant life. You can also find herbs, such as bellwort and huckleberry; shrubs, such as azaleas and mountain laurel; as well as mosses, lichens, and many other types of plants.

EXPLORE

LOOK UP

The leaves of deciduous trees come in many different shapes. They can be oval, spade-like, and even triangular. But they do have at least one thing in common: All the leaves are broad. This allows them to capture as much sunlight as possible for photosynthesis. Go on a leaf-hunting expedition. How many different deciduous leaves can you find?

LOOK AROUND

One of the most well-known deciduous trees of the northeastern United States and Canada is the sugar maple tree. People use the tree's sap to make maple syrup in the spring. That's when the warmer climate causes pressure to build up inside the tree. This pressure pushes sugary sap that's been stored deep inside the trunk upward. People access the sap by drilling a small hole into the trunk. Are there any sugar maple trees where you live? Look for these clues: small, wing-shaped fruits in the spring and bright red leaves in the fall.

ANIMALS

Deciduous forests are home to many insects. One in particular, *Aphaenogaster rudis*, a species of ant, helps the forest grow. The ants carry fallen plant seeds back to their nests in nutrient-rich soils. There, they feed them to growing larvae, which eat parts of the seed, but leave the embryo alone. Over time, the seed embryo, helped by the rich soil, is able to grow into a tree.

HAVE FUN

Get a group of friends together for a fun nature ID game. Bring some paper and pencils too. First, gather five or six different nature objects such as a rock, leaf, stick, or pinecone. Designate one person to be the person who passes each object at the start of the game. Have everyone else stand in a circle with their eyes closed. The passer will then give the first object to one person in the circle. That person will feel the object and pass it on. Keep going until everyone has had a chance to feel the object. Once the passer has the object back and puts it down with the other objects, everyone opens their eyes and writes down what they thought the object was. Repeat this until you have passed all the objects around. Then see who got the most correct answers!

fun fact

More than 200 species of squirrels live in forests on every continent except Australia and Antarctica.

DECIDUOUS FORESTS in all seasons

SPRING

In the spring, days become longer—which means more sunlight. During this time, a green pigment inside the leaves called chlorophyll captures the sun's energy. This energy is used to power a chemical reaction that converts carbon dioxide and water in the plant into sugar. This process is called photosynthesis. Deciduous trees—and other plants—use the sugar to fuel growth, make flowers, produce fruit, and power other life processes.

SUMMER

In summer, forests are in full bloom. Trees produce more sugar than they need—but they won't let it go to waste. Instead, they store the sugar as starch inside their bark. They'll use this surplus to survive in the cold winter, when sunlight is limited and they are unable to make food through photosynthesis. They also use the extra sugar to produce buds at the end of the summer. The buds stay dormant until the spring, when they are ready to open.

Trees that grow in Earth's temperate regions experience four seasons: winter, spring, summer, and fall. Although some trees that grow in temperate zones experience little change throughout the year, others undergo transformations with almost every season. These trees are known as deciduous trees, and they are found in the United States, Canada, Europe, Russia, China, and Japan.

FALL

In the fall, the number of daylight hours decreases. With less sunlight, chlorophyll breaks down and the leaves' green color fades. Soon, the leaves' true colors are revealed: Poplar and birch trees have yellow leaves; scarlet oaks have dark red leaves; dogwood leaves are purple; and sugar maple leaves are bright red and orange. Pine, spruce, and other coniferous trees stay green all year. That's why they are nicknamed "evergreen" trees.

WINTER

As fall ends, another change takes place. A layer of cells develops in each leaf's stem. Eventually, these cells cut off the stem from the tree, causing the leaf to fall. By winter, most of the leaves have fallen and the trees are bare. They will remain this way until spring, when the cycle begins again. Winter is also the time when tree roots serve as a food storage area so trees are ready to produce leaves and flowers when spring returns.

Make a FAiRY (OR GNOME!) HOUSE

WE IMAGINE FAIRIES HANGING OUT UNDER THE CAP of a toadstool, but you can create your own cozy spot to entice the forest fairies—or gnomes—to come pay a visit. Use bits of nature found in the woods to create the perfect habitat.

fun fact

What are toadstools? They're mushrooms with a fancy name. Mushrooms don't have chlorophyll—the green pigment in grass—so they don't need light to grow. That's why you can find them in dark, shady forests—and even in caves. (Some mushrooms are poisonous, so remember not to pick them!)

SUPPLY LIST

- Sticks, pebbles, moss, pieces of bark, pinecones, and grasses
- Craft glue
- Popsicle sticks

STEPS

1. Go on a nature walk with the specific mission of collecting building materials for your fairy or gnome house. Bark, pinecones, grasses, and moss would work well as materials.
2. Using craft glue, start assembling! Fairies and gnomes are tiny, so your house doesn't need to be much higher than both of your fists stacked. For a gnome house you may want to make it a bit bigger.
3. Find a cozy location for your house. Since you're using mainly natural materials, your fairy or gnome house will blend right in with the woods. Don't forget to lay down a "cobblestone" path of pebbles.
4. If you build your house in the spring, make another in the fall. Different seasons bring different building supplies—and a new look for a home!

Time: about 1 hour

THE BROTHERS GRIMM

The brothers Grimm, who published collections of folk tales about Hansel and Gretel, Snow White, Little Red Riding Hood, and others in the early 19th century, didn't make the stories up themselves. They collected the stories that had been handed down for generations and put them in books. Their books were originally written for adults, not kids!

Name that ANiMAL TRACK

You may not see all the animals that are in the woods, but you can find signs of them by looking for their tracks. Look for animal tracks near sources of food—like berry bushes—or water. Winter is an especially good time to go scouting for tracks—snow acts as a blank canvas for animals to pitter-patter across! Can you identify these animal tracks?

A

This five-inch-wide (13 cm) paw print with four toes above the pad belongs to one oversized kitty.

B

These tracks belong to a large furry creature with five toes on each paw. Its hind feet are wider, but shorter than a grown human's, but its claws are much sharper.

C

The five fingers that belong to this masked creature are capable of turning knobs and opening jars!

fun fact

One of the largest animal tracks ever discovered was that of a long-necked, plant-eating dinosaur. It was found in France and measured 4.9 feet (1.5 m) in diameter. This suggested that the dinosaur was about 82 feet (25 m) long!

D

The prints to this black, feathered creature may be found on the ground, but you listen for its caw overhead.

F

The front feet of this track are about as wide as a quarter, but the back feet (which are made for hopping) are three times that long.

E

If you follow these paw prints, which look like something flat is being dragged between them, you might find yourself at a gnawed-down tree.

A. Mountain lion; **B.** Black bear; **C.** Raccoon; **D.** Crow; **E.** American beaver; **F.** Eastern cottontail rabbit

Make a LEAF OR BARK RUBBiNG

HAVE YOU EVER MADE A LEAF OR BARK RUBBING before? Go for a walk through the woods. Notice similarities and differences among the trees and leaves around you. Choose your favorite tree and two or three leaves. Then follow the steps on the next page to take a reminder of the forest home with you.

fun fact

People have chewed on hardened tree resin as gum for thousands of years!

SUPPLY LIST

- Several large pieces of paper
- Crayons, charcoal, or oil pastels

STEPS

1. Find a tree with interesting bark and some leaves with fun shapes. Spread your paper flat against the bark or over a leaf. Using the side of your crayon, charcoal, or oil pastel, rub up and down. The pattern of the bark or leaf will appear.
2. Switch colors. Do different colors show off the texture of the bark or leaf better?
3. Compare different barks and leaves by doing more rubbings.
4. You can do rubbings of your own backyard trees and leaves. Then hang up your rubbings for your very own art show!

Time: about 10 minutes

WHAT DOES TREE BARK DO?

Bark is a tree's suit of armor. Bark protects trees from weather, fire, and insects that may damage them. The bark that you rubbed for your artwork is made from dead cells. Underneath is the inner bark, which is made of living cells that help transport food from the leaves to other parts of the tree.

RAIN FORESTS

Rain forests are located in areas that receive more than 70 inches (178 cm) of rainfall each year. There are two types of rain forests: temperate and tropical.

Temperate rain forests occur in coastal areas between the tropical and polar regions. Tongass National Forest in Alaska is the world's largest temperate rain forest.

Tropical rain forests grow near the Equator, in areas such as South and Central America, West Africa, and Southeast Asia. The world's largest is the Amazon Rain Forest in South America. It covers as much land as the 48 contiguous U.S. states!

EXPLORE

LISTEN UP

In a rain forest, the upper parts of trees grow closely together and form the forest's ceiling, or canopy. These leafy surroundings can make it difficult for the birds and monkeys that live there to see each other, so they must rely on verbal communication to get by. If you're in a rain forest, close your eyes and tune in. Can you hear any howls, whistles, or shrills?

LOOK DOWN

Life in a rain forest isn't just challenging for the animals; plants in a densely packed canopy must also come up with clever ways to obtain the resources they need to survive. The strangler fig tree, found in tropical rain forests, grows from seeds that have been dispersed on high branches of trees. The seeds shoot roots down to the forest floor. These roots slowly "strangle" the older tree from which they grow by soaking up most of the water and nutrients from the ground.

ANIMALS

Animal life isn't limited to just the canopies of temperate and tropical rain forests. Birds, such as macaws and bald eagles, can be found above the canopy, in treetops that reach 130 feet (40 m) above the ground. Big cats, such as jaguars and clouded leopards, dwell in the understory, an area just below the canopy. Meanwhile, the forest floor is home to insects, mammals, and amphibians.

HAVE FUN

Grab a camera and snap photos of some of the unusual sights you see. Experiment with camera angles by getting down on your stomach or climbing a tree and shooting downward. You may also want to experiment with natural light. Sunlight shining through a dense canopy can speckle the trees with uneven light, so you may find that the best time to take photos is when the skies are cloudy. After you're done, you can share your favorite pictures with the world by uploading them to NG Kids My Shot at kids-myshot .nationalgeographic.com.

fun fact

Giant rodents called capybaras live in the Amazon rain forest. The rodents stand up to 25 inches (64 cm) at the shoulders. That's about as tall as some German shepherds!

Make a TERRARIUM

COLLECT MATERIALS FROM THE GREAT OUTDOORS SO you can enjoy nature when you're back inside. A terrarium is a great way to experiment with plants on a miniature level.

fun fact

Mosses grow in damp environments and are home to a little creature called a moss piglet! Moss piglets have eight legs and grow up to about 1.5 millimeters in length.

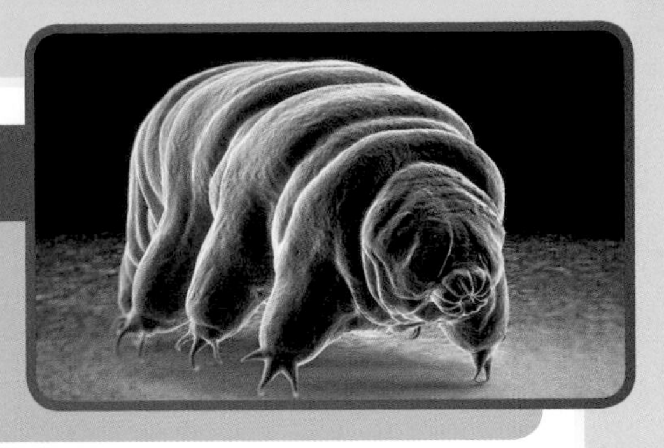

SUPPLY LIST

- Fishbowl or jar
- Activated charcoal
- Potting soil
- A variety of plants (miniature ferns or spider moss) or seeds (such as sweet alyssum or wheatgrass)
- Bits of nature from the outdoors such as leaves, twigs, and mosses

STEPS

1. Wash and dry a large glass bowl or jar. (An old fishbowl works well.)
2. Fill the bottom—about 1 inch (2.5 cm) high—with stones you have collected from your nature hikes.
3. Using a shovel or spoon, add several inches of potting soil mixed with activated charcoal bits.
4. If you are using potted plants, dig a little hole in the soil for the roots and place the plants in. Pack extra soil around the plants. Add water until the soil is moist. (If you're using seeds, press them into the soil and moisten.)
5. Add sheet moss on top of the soil around the plants.
6. Now the fun part! Add a few decorative bits of nature—a small pinecone, a special rock, or a little figurine. Keep your terrarium in a well-lit place, and don't forget to add a little water when the soil looks dry.

Time: about 30 minutes

HOW DO PLANTS BREATHE?

Humans take in oxygen when we breathe in and release carbon dioxide when we breathe out. Plants work the opposite way—they take in carbon dioxide and release oxygen. So how many houseplants would it take to replace all the oxygen you use in an hour? Scientists estimate between 300 and 500!

Name that REPTILE OR AMPHIBIAN

What's the difference between an amphibian and a reptile? One of the major differences is almost all reptiles have scales, but amphibians do not (even though some are kind of bumpy). Can you identify these amphibians and reptiles?

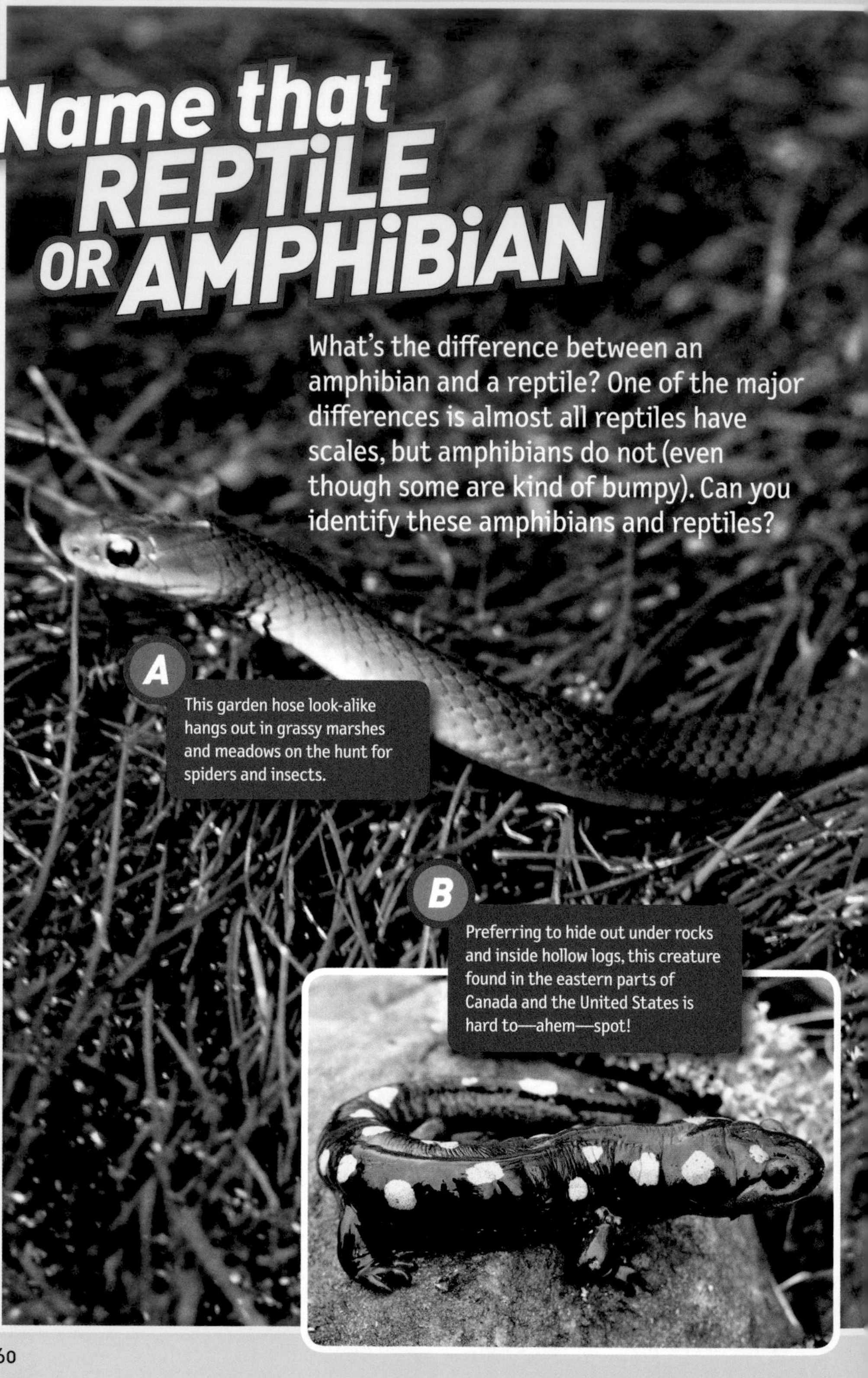

A

This garden hose look-alike hangs out in grassy marshes and meadows on the hunt for spiders and insects.

B

Preferring to hide out under rocks and inside hollow logs, this creature found in the eastern parts of Canada and the United States is hard to—ahem—spot!

C

This slow mover is about the size of your hand and will eat just about anything that it comes across. Despite its name, it is not square-shaped, but rather its shell looks like a dome.

D

You can name this hopper by looking at the underside of its legs and belly.

E

With a triangle-shaped head and a venomous bite, this creature makes its presence known with a shake of its tail.

fun fact

Snakes never stop growing! They shed their skin (called molting) after new skin has formed underneath. They keep getting bigger—little by little—their whole lives.

F

While it looks like it just walked out of the Jurassic period, this animal snatches up prey in lakes and rivers in the southeastern U.S.

A. Smooth green snake; **B.** Spotted salamander; **C.** Box turtle; **D.** California red-legged frog; **E.** Mojave rattlesnake; **F.** Alligator snapping turtle

GET OUTSIDE with National Geographic EXPLORERS

Buuveibaatar Bayarbaatar, Biologist

Buuveibaatar Bayarbaatar is a biologist from the Selenge province in Mongolia. After finishing his master's degree in biology, Buuveibaatar joined a saiga conservation project with the Wildlife Conservation Society. He now dedicates his life to saving the endangered saiga, a type of antelope that lives in Mongolia and some other parts of Asia. Buuveibaatar spends his summers traveling the Mongolian steppes to monitor and collect data on these amazing mammals that he describes as "odd-looking with unusual bulbous noses."

www.nationalgeographic.com/explorers/bios/buuveibaatar-bayarbaatar

Dana Bunnell-Young, Environmental Scientist

As a kid, Dana Bunnell-Young grew up kayaking, fishing, and observing the wildlife in her home state of Delaware, U.S.A. Inspired by a childhood spent on the water, Dana is now devoted to finding solutions to the environmental difficulties that the Chesapeake Bay and other waterways face today. She is committed to protecting the environment and cleaning up local rivers and streams so that future generations may continue to enjoy the water and all its wonderful wildlife!

www.nationalgeographic.com/explorers/bios/dana-bunnell-young

Mariana Fuentes, Marine Biologist/Ecologist

A marine biologist and ecologist from Brazil, Mariana Fuentes specializes in the conservation and management of sea turtles. Inspired by the turtles' "beauty, persistence, [and] strength," Mariana hopes to contribute to turtles' ongoing survival through community involvement and education. Though Mariana's work has taken her from Australia to Barbados, her favorite experience is still watching sea turtle hatchlings emerge from their nests.

www.nationalgeographic.com/explorers/bios/mariana-fuentes

Isabelle Charrier, Biologist

Growing up, Isabelle Charrier wanted to be a veterinarian to better understand animal behavior. These days, she studies vocal communication in pinnipeds—fin-footed mammals such as seals, sea lions, and walruses. A normal day for Isabelle involves working closely with pinnipeds to record their social interactions within their natural environments. She believes that studying the ways in which these animals communicate can help us better protect them and their environments. Her favorite experience in the field was spending nine months studying fur seals!

www.nationalgeographic.com/explorers/bios/isabelle-charrier

EXPLORE YOUR
BACKYARD

BACKYARDS AROUND THE WORLD

Gardening has been a favorite pastime for thousands of years. In ancient Egypt, people grew palms and acacias around lotus ponds, while in Persia people created "paradise gardens"—walled pools and vegetation in otherwise barren areas. Today, people use gardens of the past for inspiration when designing their own landscape. Check out these famous gardens from around the world. Maybe you can use them to inspire a garden of your own.

GARDEN MAZE, LURAY CAVERNS

Garden mazes, which are styled from tall hedges, evolved from the knot gardens of Europe in the 1500s. The Garden Maze at Luray Caverns in Virginia is made from 1,500 dark American arborvitae bushes that stand eight feet (2.4 m) tall. The maze twists and turns at 40 points, so it's no surprise that finding a way out of the maze can be difficult. Fortunately, visitors can climb up a lookout tower to figure out where they are.

KENROKU-EN GARDEN

It is believed that the Kenroku-en garden in Kanazawa, Japan, was completed in about 1632. It is home to one of the oldest water fountains in Japan and a teahouse that was built in 1775. There are more than 8,500 trees to see and more than 180 species of plants! Want to see some animals? There are lots of koi in beautiful ponds around the garden's grounds.

ROYAL VICTORIA PARK

In the early 1800s, many English people planted different colored flowers in their gardens. They arranged the flowers in a way that made them look like patterns of an ornate carpet or rug. This was called "carpet bedding." The Royal Victoria Park garden in Bath, England, is a great place to see this type of gardening with all of its colorful flowers and beautiful trees. The garden was opened in 1830 by Princess Victoria of England when she was only 11 years old.

WALTER SISULU NATIONAL BOTANICAL GARDEN

The Walter Sisulu garden is one of eight botanical gardens in South Africa, but it isn't your typical garden. Not only does it boast many different plants from all over South Africa, it is also a haven for a number of reptiles and small mammals. There is also a waterfall and 600 species of plants. When in this garden, binoculars for bird-watching are a must! There are 220 species of birds that fly above the grounds and hang out in the trees.

WHITE HOUSE ROSE GARDEN

If you've ever watched the U.S. president give an outdoor conference on his home turf, chances are you caught a glimpse of the White House Rose Garden. The garden, which is 125 feet (38 m) long and 60 feet (18 m) wide, has been a part of the White House grounds since 1913, when it was established by First Lady Edith Roosevelt. The garden includes a variety of roses such as the "Queen Elizabeth," "Kings Ransom," and "Nevada Rose" and a few non-roses. Depending on the time of year, you might see flowers such as daffodils, tulips, and chrysanthemums.

ALL MiXED UP

Plants and animals are adapted to the conditions of the habitats in which they live. So organisms that live in areas where the climate is dry and chilly will be different from those that live in hot places with lots of rainfall. Most eastern states have warm, humid summers and moderately cold winters. Sometimes, they receive snowfall.

As you head south, things start to heat up. In Georgia and North Carolina, winter temperatures rarely dip below freezing. Meanwhile, in southern Florida, the climate is warm, wet, and tropical. So what types of plants and animals can you find in backyards of the east and south? Read on to find out.

EXPLORE

IN BLOOM

A perennial is a plant that doesn't completely die in the winter and lasts for at least two growing seasons. Their hardy quality makes perennials a popular plant in northeastern backyards and other parts of the world with similar climates. Wild ginger is an example of such a plant. It's a perennial that grows close to the ground and has fuzzy heart-shaped leaves that conceal tiny burgundy flowers in late spring. Plants that favor tropical conditions such as Elephant's ears are perfect for gardens in the southeast. Elephant's ears are water-loving plants that can grow up to 8 ft (2.4 m) tall!

MIGRATION WATCH

Depending on the time of year, you might spot a migrating animal in your backyard. The Eastern kingbird, which winters in Central and South America, migrates north to breed. The small bird, which has gray, white, and black feathers, travels in a flock and can be seen snapping up insects in midair. In addition to the Eastern kingbird, you might spot a few monarch butterflies. In the fall, the monarchs travel from Canada and the Northern United States to Mexico. Along the way they stop at nectar-bearing plants to feed. In the spring, the monarch butterflies head back north.

ANIMALS

Not all animals migrate. Some can be found in your area year-round. Trees in your yard may be a home to raccoons, opossums, Eastern screech owls, and squirrels. If you live in a damp, marshy area, keep a lookout for newts, frogs, and birds, such as cranes and egrets.

HAVE FUN

Although nectar is a butterfly's favorite food, these insects also enjoy overripe fruit like bananas, apples, peaches, and pears. You can use these fruits to create a butterfly feeder. First, take a shallow plastic container and have an adult create four holes at opposite ends near the rim. Cut four pieces of string, each about two feet (60 cm) long. Loop each piece of string through a hole in the container and then tie the loose ends together. Decorate your container with colorful stickers to mimic the nectar-filled flowers that butterflies are attracted to. Then, fill the bottom of the container with a thin layer of water and toss in some ripe pieces of fruit. Hang the container from a tree branch and wait for the butterflies to appear!

fun fact

Eastern screech owls don't just screech. They also make a trill that's similar to a horse's whinny. The owls also bark, whistle, hoot, and chuckle!

Make a TELESCOPE

IF YOU WANT A BETTER VIEW OF THE NIGHT SKY BUT don't own a telescope, you can build one of your own. Then take your new telescope out at night and gaze at the amazing night sky. See if you can name some of the constellations that you may spot!

fun fact

Tire tracks and footprints left behind by astronauts who have visited the moon will stay there forever. Why? There is no wind on the moon to blow them away!

SUPPLY LIST

- 2 paper towel tubes
- Scissors
- Masking tape
- Paint (any color you like)
- Paintbrushes
- 2 convex lenses (you can get these either from a pair of magnifying glasses or by ordering the lenses online)

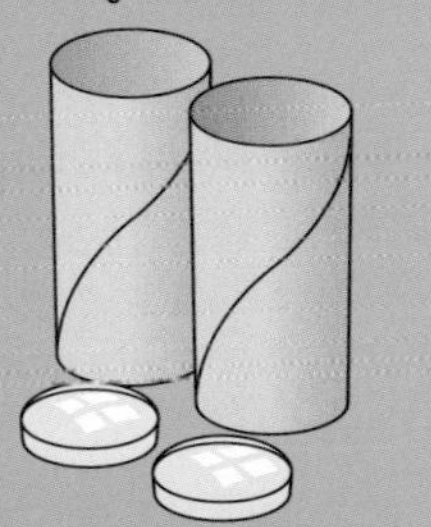

STEPS

1. Paint your paper towel tubes and let them dry.
2. Create the inner tube of the telescope. Using scissors, cut one tube lengthwise only on one side. Curl one side of the cut edge slightly over the other. Then tape the cut edge down.

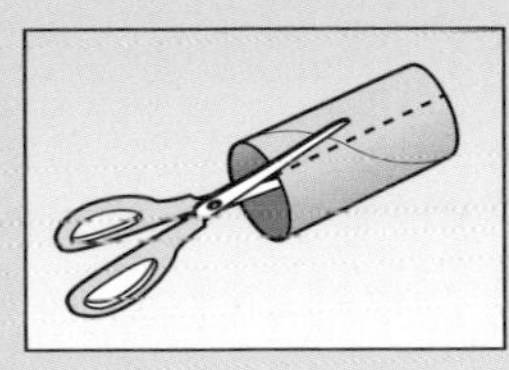

3. Insert your inner tube into the second paper towel tube. It should fit snugly into the second tube but still be able to slide in and out. If not, adjust the size of the inner tube.
4. Tape one convex lens to the outer end of each tube, only around the rim, so you don't cover too much of the lens.

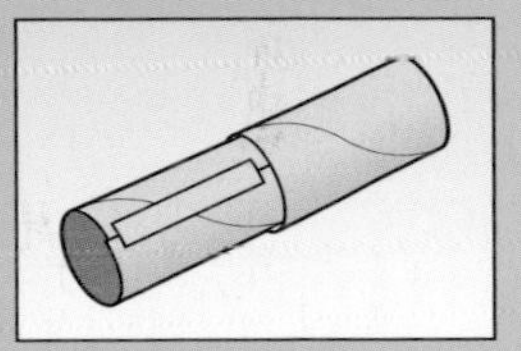

5. Hold your telescope with the inner tube facing your eye. Aim it at an object in the night sky. (Never use your telescope to look at the sun!) You can focus by sliding the inner tube in and out.

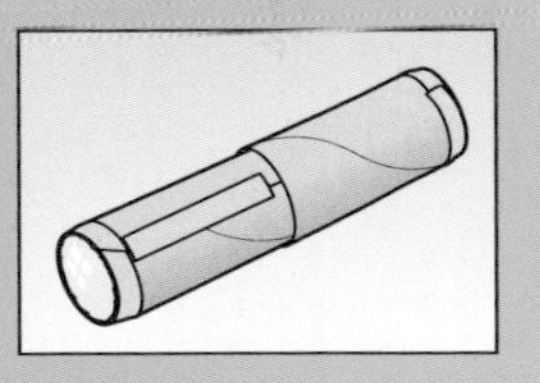

Time: about 40 minutes

HOW TO DISTINGUISH A STAR FROM A PLANET

Here's a simple trick to figure out if an object in the night sky is a star or a planet: Stars appear to "twinkle," but planets don't. Turbulence in Earth's atmosphere refracts the light from stars, making them appear to twinkle. Because planets are much closer to us than stars, they don't suffer from the turbulence the way stars do.

Constellations are clusters of stars in the sky that are grouped together in a particular pattern and have been given a name. As the Earth rotates, you can see different constellations. If you are lucky enough to live at the Equator, you can see all the constellations in a year! Can you identify the cool constellations on this page?

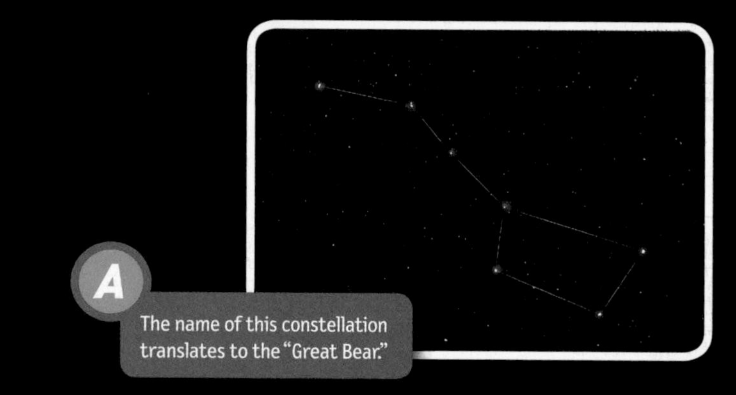

A The name of this constellation translates to the "Great Bear."

B The name of this constellation means "dragon." It also happens to be the name of Harry Potter's blond-haired nemesis.

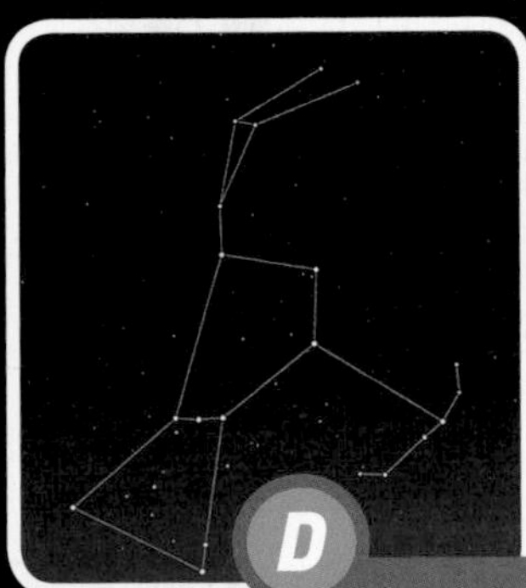

C

The strong hero in Greek mythology for whom this constellation is named is said to be holding a bow after just releasing an arrow.

D

This constellation represents the giant it is named for. He is holding a shield in front of Taurus, the bull.

E

The name of a famous winged horse is all you need to know to identify this constellation.

fun fact

Our sun is a star that's about 870,000 miles (1.4 million km) wide. That's wide enough to fit about one million Earths inside of it! The sun also makes up 99.8 percent of the mass of our solar system. That's one huge star!

F

You're not seeing double: This constellation's name means "twins" for good reason.

G

In Greek mythology, this crab (for which the constellation is named) attacked Hercules, but then met its fate when Hercules crushed it with his foot.

A. Ursa Major; **B.** Draco; **C.** Hercules; **D:** Orion; **E.** Pegasus; **F:** Gemini; **G.** Cancer

BACKYARDS in all seasons

SPRING

In the spring, you'll likely see tulips popping up in gardens across the country and around the world. Tulips were first cultivated in Turkey and were imported to Holland in the 16th century. Around that time, a botanist named Carolus Clusius wrote a book about the flower. This started a tulip-buying craze, which caused prices for tulips to skyrocket. At one point, it cost more money to buy a tulip than it did to buy a house! Fortunately, prices dropped, but appreciation for the flower did not.

SUMMER

Nothing says summer like a fresh, juicy tomato. About 60 million cans of tomatoes are produced around the world each year! While it is popular in many countries, the tomato's history can be traced to South America, where it was cultivated by the Aztec. In the 1500s, Spanish explorers brought the tomato to Europe, where it wasn't always used as food. In some parts of Italy, people believed that tomatoes were poisonous, so they used them as decorations instead.

As the seasons change, so do many backyards. What types of plants can you expect to see in a winter, spring, summer, and fall yard? Read on to find out. Then go out and discover what kinds of plants grow in your backyard and neighborhood each season. Do you see any of the plants shown below?

FALL

Can you imagine Halloween without jack-o'-lanterns or Thanksgiving without pumpkin pie? Most people can't, which explains why pumpkins are a popular fruit in the United States. But pumpkins are actually native to Central America. Pumpkin carving also has roots in other countries. Hundreds of years ago, people in Ireland carved jack-o'-lanterns out of turnips and potatoes. When Irish immigrants came to the United States, they discovered that the pumpkin worked much better.

WINTER

Thanks to its connection with Christmas, American holly may be one of the most well-known winter plants. Its small fleshy fruits—called drupes, not berries—can be black, white, yellow, and, most often, red. In addition to being used as holiday decorations, wood from holly plants has been used to make chess pieces and piano keys. Other species of holly are found all over the world. Box-leaved holly is found in China, Japan, and Korea, and English holly can be found in Europe, Asia, and Africa.

GOING TO EXTREMES

The weather of the American Midwest varies from state to state. In general, summers are hot, with temperatures soaring to 90°F (32°C) at times, while winters can be frigid; temperatures in some areas fall below 0°F (-18°C). Some parts also experience lots of snowfall. By contrast, the Southwest receives less precipitation and is much hotter. Temperatures can be as low as 40°F (4°C) in the winter but rise over 100°F (38°C) in the summer. With such extreme differences between and within these regions, it's no wonder that the backyard plant and animal life is just as varied.

EXPLORE

fun fact

The Cardon cactus, which grows in Mexico, is the tallest cactus species in the world. It can grow up to about 65 feet (20 m). Some even live for up to 200 years!

IN BLOOM

After the snow melts in the Midwest, soil is moist enough for planting and is rich in nutrients, which makes it ideal for growing crops, such as corn and wheat. The crops grow in the summer and are harvested in the fall. The American Southwest is filled with plants that are adapted to dealing with little rain and extreme heat. Plants like cacti have few or no leaves, which allows them to hold more water. Cacti also grow in deserts in South America and Africa.

ANIMALS

In the Midwest, many animals are diurnal, or active during the day. Look for black-footed ferrets, prairie dogs, box turtles, prairie falcons, and tiger salamanders. In the Southwest, where it's much hotter, many animals lurk in gardens, but few, such as the zebra-tailed lizard, will be active during the day when summer temperatures are scorching. Go out after dusk to spot animals such as jackrabbits, kangaroo rats, and banded geckos.

MIGRATION WATCH

If your midwestern backyard is near a wet grassland or field, keep an eye out for snow geese. During the winter, these birds migrate to states such as Missouri, South Dakota, and Nebraska. In early spring, they take off for the Arctic. In the Southwest, the Costas hummingbird, which has a purple crown and throat, can be spotted during the winter months, when it breeds. In the spring, the weather gets too hot for this hummingbird, so it takes off for the Pacific.

HAVE FUN

Go on a plant scavenger hunt! If you live in the Midwest, the plants in your backyard may have characteristics that are different from the plants that grow in yards of the Southwest. How many of the following plant characteristics can you find in your yard?

- Brown bark
- Hairy stems
- Flower heads that consist of many florets
- Large, wide leaves
- Long, narrow leaves
- Velvety leaves
- Flat needles
- Spines
- Thorns

Make your backyard WiLDLiFE FRiENDLY

YOU CAN INCREASE THE CHANCES THAT WILDLIFE will want to visit your backyard by making sure the plants in your yard are animal friendly. Here's a simple way to attract animals.

fun fact

Owls have small hairlike feathers on their beaks and feet to help them feel prey after it has been caught.

SUPPLY LIST

- Shrubs and bushes that are native to the area in which you live and have berries, nuts, and seeds for food. You'll want to go to a garden center with an adult and talk to the experts about what would be best.
- Birdbath (you can use the instructions on page 131!) and bird feeder (you can make one or buy one)

STEPS

1. Have an adult help you plant the shrubs and bushes around your yard. Animals may use these plants for shelter, as hiding spots, or as places to build nests. Animals that eat berries, nuts, and seeds may use them as a food source.
2. Choose an area for your birdbath and set it up with the help of an adult. Birds and maybe other small animals will use this to bathe in and to drink from.
3. Choose a tree where you can hang your bird feeder, and have an adult help you hang it up.
4. Now keep your eyes peeled for animals that come to explore your backyard. Remember not to get too close or bother the animals that visit.

Time: one afternoon

CHIPMUNKS' CHEEKS

Have you ever seen a chipmunk run by with its mouth full of acorns? Well they are able to carry large nuts, seeds, and berries in their mouths because of special pouches in their cheeks. The pouches serve not only as a way to collect lots of food, but they are also temporary storage containers. A chipmunk's pouches can expand to the size of the animal's whole body when completely full!

Name that BACKYARD ANiMAL

Sometimes animals leave signs that will let you know they've been in your backyard—like droppings or teeth marks on garden plants they've been munching! There's a chance one of these animals has visited your yard. Can you identify them?

A

With teeth that never stop growing, these bushy-tailed mammals are often munching nuts in backyard trees or dashing across telephone lines.

B

With a white, heart-shaped face, these nighttime fliers like to perch in old buildings when they aren't out hunting rodents.

C Sometimes seen using their tail for balance, these are the only marsupials found in North America.

fun fact

A skunk's spray is actually an oily substance that is produced by glands under its large, bushy tail. When a skunk is ready to spray, it can shoot the stinky substance as far as ten feet (3 m)!

E About as long as a baseball bat, these skinny reptiles aren't venomous, but they may still bite if you pick them up!

D You can identify this nocturnal creature without ever seeing it. Just follow your nose.

F Spending little time on the ground, these reptiles prefer trees—or the backyard structures that bear their name.

G They may not sing in real life, but their stripes and chubby cheeks are unmistakable.

A. Squirrel; **B.** Barn owl; **C.** Opossum; **D.** Skunk; **E.** Common garter snake; **F.** Eastern fence lizard; **G.** Chipmunk

TAKE TIME TO STOP AND PICK THE DANDELIONS!

Sitting in the grass and picking flowers is relaxing, but stringing them together into a chain is downright entertaining. When you're outside, pick some flowers for an instant accessory! Be sure you are allowed to pick the flowers before you begin.

fun fact

Moonflower is the name of a group of flowering plants that only bloom at night. Some only bloom once a year for a single night.

ANCIENT PERFUMES

In 2005, archaeologists on the Mediterranean island of Cyprus uncovered what are believed to be the oldest perfumes in the world in an ancient perfumery that dates back 4,000 years. Many years ago it is believed that people made perfumes out of spices, herbs, almonds, and flowers, among other ingredients.

SUPPLY LIST

- Flowers, especially daisies or dandelions. Plain and simple! Nothing else is needed.

STEPS

1. Find a patch of dandelions or daisies and start picking! (Ask permission if they aren't yours!) The stem should be about half the length of your index finger.

2. Using your fingernail, split the stem making a small slit about 1/4 inch (6 mm) long.

3. Slide a second flower stem-first through the slit until the flower head is at the hole.

4. Repeat steps two and three until you reach the desired length.

5. To finish your chain, make a second slit in the first flower and slip the last flower through it.

Time: 20 minutes or more

RAIN AND SHINE

The western part of the United States is diverse in climate. Up north, the weather may be warm and dry in the summer, but it's usually cool and damp during the rest of the year. Farther south, summer and winter are mild along the coast, but when you travel inland to desert areas, the climate becomes more extreme; temperatures are scorching hot in the summer and cold in the winter. Meanwhile, the climate in Hawaii is tropical. Since the climates in these areas vary greatly, so do the plants and animals that live there.

EXPLORE

IN BLOOM

There are more than 180 species of trees in the American West, the most well-known being redwoods. And while you may not have one of these 275-foot (84 m) giants growing in your backyard, you will likely see oak trees and poppies. In addition, succulents—plants that store water in enlarged cells and can go for long periods of time without rainfall—are found along the West Coast. Hawaii's damp tropical climate makes it an ideal place for fruit-bearing plants such as pineapple and mango, as well as flower-producing plants such as the yellow hibiscus.

ANIMALS

Western gray squirrels can be found in the trees of the western United States and Canada. Other inhabitants include the stellar's jay, the California newt, the banded forest snail, the northern Pacific rattlesnake, and the Indian mongoose in Hawaii.

MIGRATION WATCH

If you live in the West, don't be surprised to see a mule deer grazing on your lawn. During the summer, mule deer populations reside in mountainous regions. But in the winter, snow covers the ground—and their food supply. So, the deer must move to lower woodlands, where there is little or no snow. Along the way, the deer may stop at farms and other residential areas to rest—and feed. If you are along the coastlines of Alaska and Hawaii, you might spy a humpback whale. In the summer, many whales cruise around their grounds in the Gulf of Alaska, but in the winter, they may head to the warm tropical waters around the Hawaiian islands to give birth.

HAVE FUN

No matter where your backyard is, you can adopt your own tree! Get permission to go on a nature walk within a close-by and familiar area. Take a look around at the trees that are near you. Choose one to observe and take a closer look at it. Touch it, smell it, and listen to the leaves swaying in the wind. Think about how your tree is similar and different from the other trees and plants around you. Keep a nature journal about the observations you've made and come back to your tree each season and in different weather conditions to see how it has changed. What do you notice?

fun fact

Male mule deer, called bucks, have large antlers made of living tissue. Each year, the bucks shed their antlers in winter and regrow them in spring.

Make a PRESSED FLOWER

A BEAUTIFUL, PICKED FLOWER LASTS A FEW DAYS.
A pressed one can last years! Follow these steps to preserve your favorite flower. When you're done, glue it to a piece of paper and frame it. You will have created a piece of art worth sharing!

fun fact

The oldest flower fossil ever discovered was found in China in 2002. The flower, named *Archaefructus sinensis*, is believed to have bloomed 125 million years ago!

SUPPLY LIST

- Fresh picked flowers
- A few tissues
- Heavy books

STEPS

1. Pick a few bright, colorful flowers. (Make sure they aren't wet.) Thin flowers, such as forget-me-nots, daisies, or violets, work best. Thick flowers, like roses, are harder to press, but you can pick a few petals and just press those.
2. Arrange your flowers on a piece of tissue. You may keep the stems on or remove them. Place another tissue on top.
3. Open a heavy book, like a large dictionary. Place your tissue-covered flowers in the middle of a page. Pigment from some flowers can bleed. You may want to put some plain paper down on each side of the tissue to protect your book.
4. Firmly close the book, then stack several more heavy books on top of it. The pressing process has started!
5. Thin, delicate flowers should remain in the book for at least two weeks. Larger flowers should stay in four to six weeks. When they are dry and perfectly flat, they're done!

Time: about five minutes, plus six weeks to allow the flower to be pressed properly

AN ART AS OLD AS THE PHARAOHS

Drying and pressing flowers has been in practice for thousands of years: Dried flowers have been found in ancient Egyptian tombs. In Victorian times, women used dried flowers to decorate artwork. Since the 16th century, Japanese artists have been making beautiful pressed flower art, called *oshibana*.

Name that WiLDFLOWER

Flowers come in many shapes, sizes, and colors and are found all over the world. Can you identify the wildflowers on this page? When you're done, go outside and see if you can identify the flowers where you live.

A

The first part of this flower's name is the same as its color. The second part is the word for that crispy, crunchy thing that holds your ice cream.

B

The name of this stunning flower is a compound word. The first word is another way of saying "angry" and the second may make you think of growing grapes.

C

This lovely lavender flower is abundant in North America. The first part of its name is the same as a honey-loving insect.

D

The name of these tiny clustered flowers includes their color and a popular drink that helps bones grow.

E

This flower is native to Europe and Asia. Part of its name includes a word that means the opposite of "remember."

F

This unique flower is native to western North America and is named for its deep and vivid color, which is another word that describes the color red.

fun fact

The flower with the world's largest bloom—*Rafflesia arnoldii*—is commonly known as the monster flower, and it smells of rotting flesh! Up to three feet (about 1 m) across, the monster flower's fragrance and color—which is pinkish red, like meat—attract flies and beetles as pollinators.

A. Purple coneflower; **B.** Crossvine flower; **C.** Bee balm; **D.** Pink milkweed wildflower; **E.** Water forget-me-not; **F.** Crimson columbine

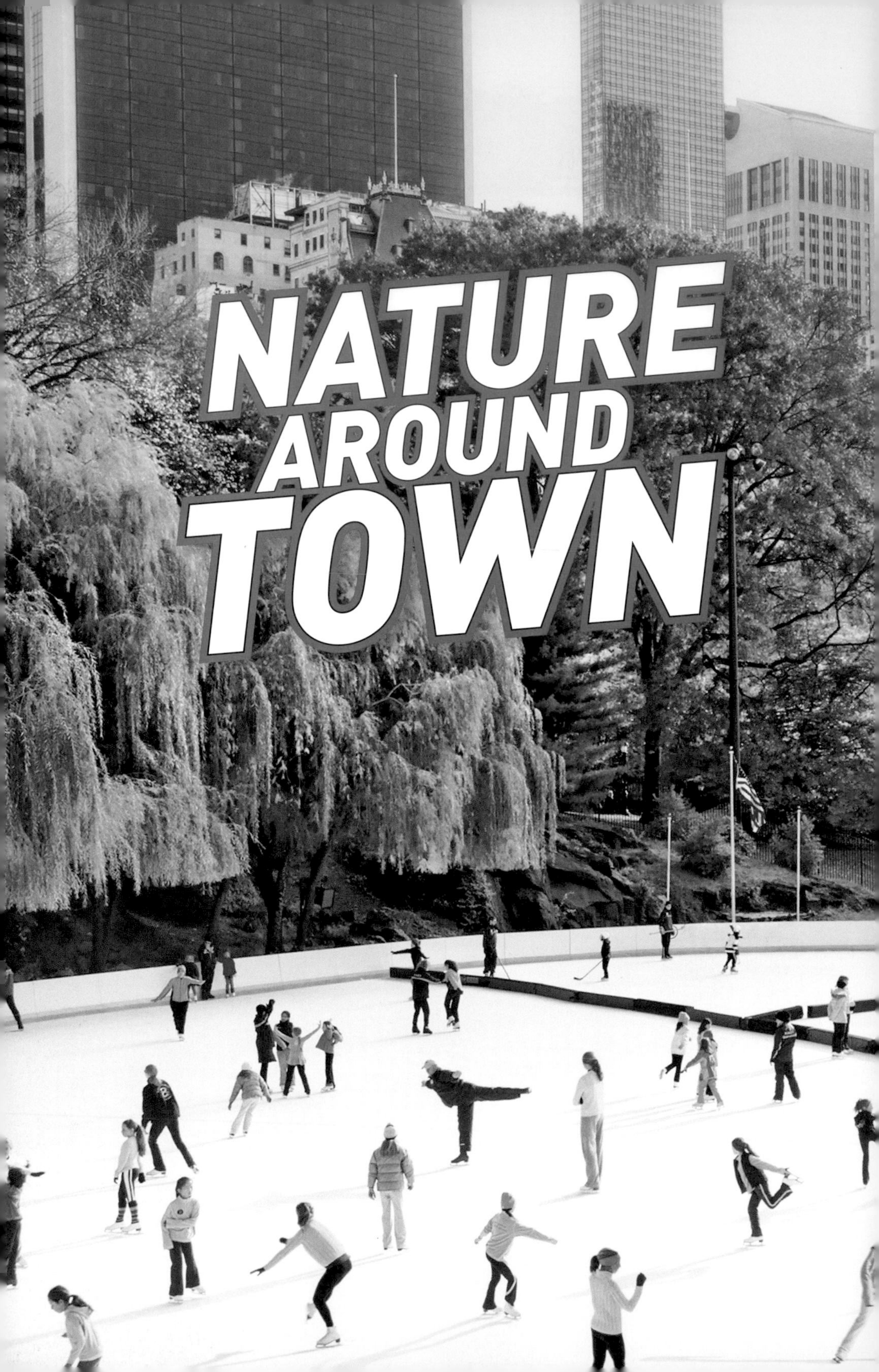
NATURE
AROUND
TOWN

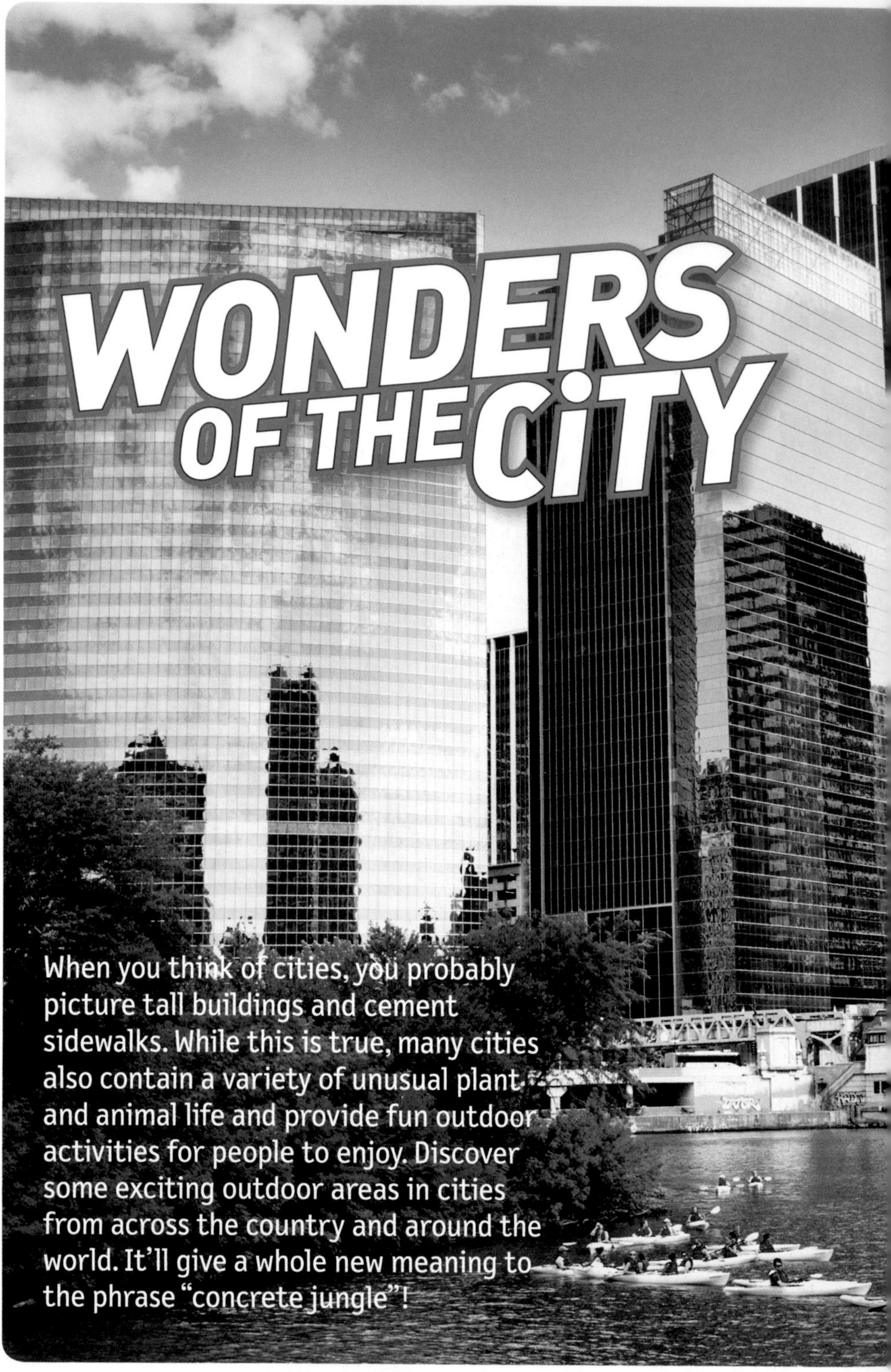

WONDERS OF THE CITY

When you think of cities, you probably picture tall buildings and cement sidewalks. While this is true, many cities also contain a variety of unusual plant and animal life and provide fun outdoor activities for people to enjoy. Discover some exciting outdoor areas in cities from across the country and around the world. It'll give a whole new meaning to the phrase "concrete jungle"!

URBAN JUNGLE

An outdoor jungle adventure right in the middle of Sydney, Australia! That's where you will find this very cool and very large playground. Located on the grounds of the Sydney Olympic Park, this urban oasis is full of high ropes and climbing courses that take you off the ground and into the trees. Adventurers can choose from 5 different courses and 50 different activities, and it's fun for kids and grown-ups alike!

FISHERMAN'S WHARF

If you head to Pier 39 of San Francisco's Fisherman's Wharf, you'll be greeted by an unusual city sight: hundreds of sea lions basking in the sun! The sea lions have always been around San Francisco Bay, but it wasn't until 1989 that they began flocking to the pier. Many people believe that a powerful earthquake that occurred around that time scared the sea lions, so they headed to the pier where they felt safer.

THE HIGH LINE

Sometimes city parks can be found in the most unusual places. New York City's High Line was once an elevated outdoor railroad. The railroad had been unused since 1980 and was going to be demolished. Over the years, community residents rallied to have the railroad turned into a public space and eventually succeeded. In 2009, the High Line park opened. The park contains 210 species of plants and extends one mile (1.6 km) along the city's west side.

DANUBE ISLAND

Even in a bustling city like Vienna, Austria, there is a special place to truly enjoy nature and the outdoors. Danube Island is a narrow strip of land that separates one side of the Danube River from the other. The island is home to a water playground that features a waterfall, a bridge, and a sandpit. The area is surrounded by trees and is along the banks of one of the longest rivers in Europe. The water for the swimming pond comes directly from the river itself, and it's a great place to spot a variety of wildlife, too!

GEORGIA AQUARIUM

Who says you have to go deep-sea diving to find marine life? The Georgia Aquarium in Atlanta, Georgia, is home to 120,000 marine and freshwater animals! These include bottlenose dolphins, manta rays, whale sharks, sea otters, black-footed penguins, and leafy sea dragons. To help the different animal species feel at home, the aquarium has re-created more than 60 natural habitats, ranging from arctic to tropical waters.

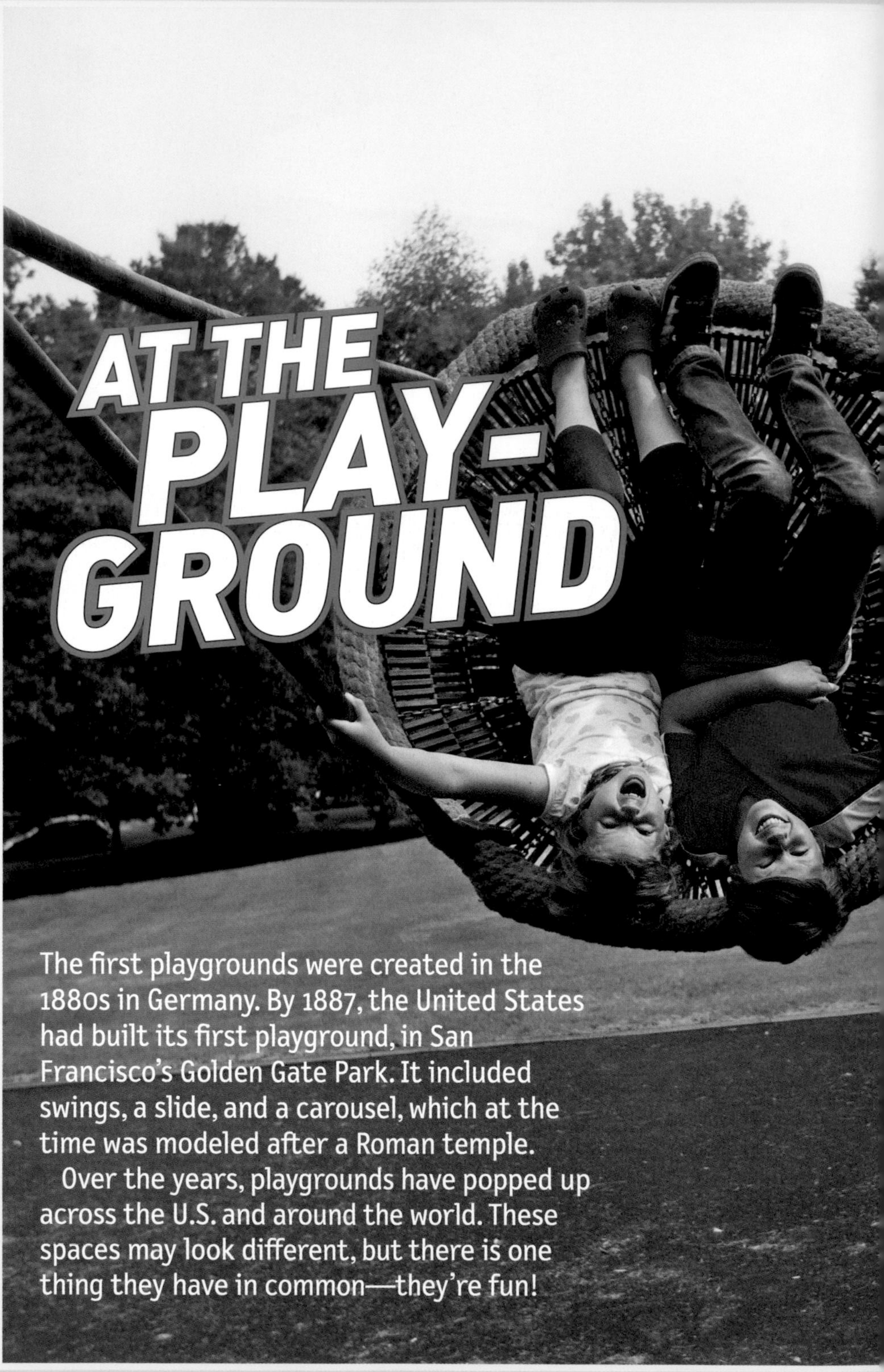

AT THE PLAY-GROUND

The first playgrounds were created in the 1880s in Germany. By 1887, the United States had built its first playground, in San Francisco's Golden Gate Park. It included swings, a slide, and a carousel, which at the time was modeled after a Roman temple.

Over the years, playgrounds have popped up across the U.S. and around the world. These spaces may look different, but there is one thing they have in common—they're fun!

EXPLORE

LOOK AROUND

What does the playground in your city look like? If it has plastic slides and metal jungle gyms, it may be ready for a makeover. New playgrounds—called "natural playscapes"—feature elements from nature in their designs. Kids can climb up boulders and logs, hop from one tree stump to another, or zip down a slide that's built into a grassy hill. The makers of these new playscapes hope their designs will bring more nature into urban environments.

LOOK DOWN

Even if the surface of your playground has more concrete than green, you can still find plant life. One plant in particular—the dandelion—is very common. It can be found growing among grasses as well as through the cracks of sidewalks. How do dandelions get there? After pollination, a dandelion's bright yellow petals turn to white fuzzy seeds that are easily spread around—often blown by wind or people making wishes. The seeds often grow in places where they land. Now go find a dandelion and make a wish!

ANIMALS

Depending on the city you live in, you can find many different birds and insects in your playground. One animal that's likely common to most playgrounds is the tree squirrel. Tree squirrels are bushy-tailed rodents with terrific climbing abilities. Though they live in trees, they come to the ground often in search of nuts, acorns, berries, and flowers. How many squirrels can you spot in your playground?

fun fact

The word "dandelion"comes from the French phrase *dent de lion*. The phrase means "lion's tooth," which is what some people thought a dandelion leaf looked like.

HAVE FUN

Challenge your friends to a playground scavenger hunt! All you need is a timer and the list below. Set your timer for five minutes and then begin searching for the items on the list. Check off each item as you find it. When the time is up, compare your lists. The person who checked off the most items wins.

- A spiderweb
- Something green
- A ball
- A furry animal
- A bird
- An insect
- Something made from wood
- Sand
- Water
- A bicycle

Make an ICE SUN CATCHER

WHEN THE COLD WINTER DAYS ARRIVE, GO OUTSIDE and decorate! Dangle a natural ice sculpture in your yard, at school, or leave one as a treat for your neighbors. Just like a snowflake, no two sun catchers are alike. Get creative!

fun fact

To survive a cold winter, the wood frog has antifreeze-like blood to keep from freezing solid. Its heart stops beating and doesn't revive until it thaws in warm weather!

DREAM CATCHERS

Have you ever seen a dream catcher? Some Native American cultures made dream catchers by creating a hoop out of bark and weaving a web onto it with string. Then they would add items they believed were sacred. These included feathers and beads. Native Americans believed that dream catchers would rid bad dreams and only allow good ones to come to them when they were sleeping. Today dream catchers are a popular decoration among people outside of the Native American community.

SUPPLY LIST

- Bundt pan
- Bits of nature such as small pebbles and twigs, leaves, and berries
- Ribbon or string
- Water

STEPS

1. Fill a Bundt pan half full of water. (If you don't have a Bundt pan, fill an 8-inch (20 cm) cake pan halfway with water and place an empty yogurt container in the middle, which will help form the ring.)
2. Gather bits of nature: Things like pine needles, pinecones, red leaves, and berries work well. Arrange them in the pan.
3. Put the pan in the freezer until frozen solid. Pop the sculpture out of the pan and loop a ribbon through the ring. Hang it from a branch and enjoy!

Time: about 20 minutes, plus freezing time

Name that MOON PHASE

Ever since you were old enough to point you've probably picked out the moon in the sky. And you've probably noticed with each passing day, the moon changes just a little bit. The moon goes through eight phases in a 29.5-day cycle because it orbits Earth. This causes the illuminated part that we see to gradually change. Can you name these moon phases?

A

The moon is more than half full, but we haven't seen its full face yet.

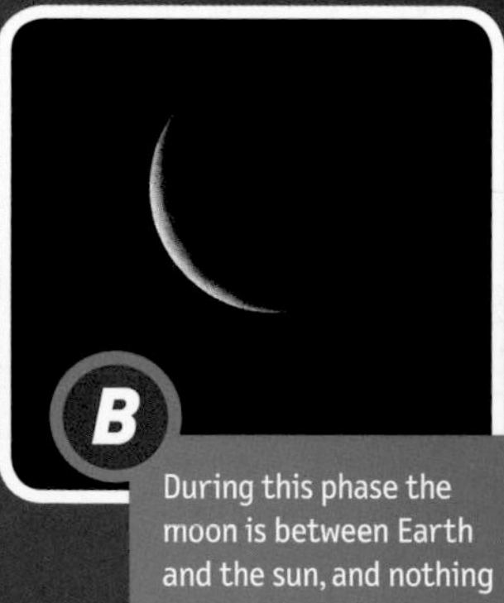

B

During this phase the moon is between Earth and the sun, and nothing appears to be lit.

C

A sliver of the moon is visible, and it is a little bit bigger than it was the night before.

D

The moon is behind Earth from the perspective of the sun.

fun fact

The moon has earthquakes just like Earth does, except they're called moonquakes. Although moonquakes are not as strong as most powerful earthquakes here, they last much longer. Some can shake for one hour or more.

E

This is the last phase before the moon is new again.

F

Just past its full-moon glory, this moon is getting smaller each night.

G

We can see half of the moon again. But we'll see less of it the next night.

A. Waxing gibbous; **B.** New moon; **C.** Waxing crescent; **D.** Full moon; **E.** Waning crescent; **F.** Waning gibbous; **G.** Third quarter

CiTiES in all seasons

SPRING

Each spring, many visitors and residents of Washington, D.C., flock to the Potomac River to catch sight of the blooming cherry blossom trees. Many of the trees were donated to the city in 1912 as a symbol of friendship by Mayor Yukio Ozaki of Tokyo, Japan. Since then, the trees have been a major attraction. The city celebrates the blooms with a three-week festival that includes performances, a parade, and art exhibits. When the flower petals fall, the green grass is covered in pink. It's a nice sight to see!

SUMMER

In June, architects, designers, and engineers hit the beach in Galveston, Texas, where they compete in an annual sand castle contest. Using sand, water, and their imaginations, contestants sculpt sharks, lizards, buildings, and even scenes from movies and history in an effort to win the grand prize: the Gold Bucket Award. Sand-sculpting festivals are also held in other countries, including Australia, Portugal, and Turkey.

Many cities across the United States and the world host special events throughout the year. The events, which range from festivals to competitions, are a huge hit with locals and visitors and are a great way to ring in the changing seasons. Check out a few of these festivities below.

FALL

Many cities host Halloween events in the fall. One of the most unique events is the Tompkins Square Park Halloween Dog Parade in New York City. Each October, dog owners dress up their pooches in Halloween costumes and then parade them around the park. The dog with the best costume wins a prize. In the past, costumes have included pumpkins, tacos, cell phones, and a plate of spaghetti! Halloween has also become popular in other parts of the world, including Japan and Hong Kong.

WINTER

In Fairbanks, Alaska, people venture outside in the cold to enjoy the city's World Ice Art Championships. The event attracts sculptors from across the globe who chisel and saw giant blocks of ice into whimsical forms such as dragons and mermaids. The event dates back to 1934, when locals staged their first winter carnival. To prepare for the event, water was poured over wooden chairs and allowed to freeze. The frozen chairs served as ice thrones for the carnival king and queen.

AT THE ZOO

You may not encounter many wild animals while walking down a city sidewalk, but you can view and learn about them at your local zoo. Zoos are places where people can safely interact with animals that typically live in the wild. The first modern zoos appeared in the 1700s. Today, zookeepers and planners take special measures to make sure that the animals are comfortable and safe. They re-create the animals' natural habitats and feed them the right foods. Read on to discover more about zoos!

EXPLORE

LET'S EAT

Animals that live in the wild hunt or forage for food. But zoo animals rely on zookeepers to feed them. Zookeepers must know each animal's food preferences and dietary needs so that they can keep the animals healthy. For example, a chimpanzee's menu may consist of fruit, such as apples and oranges, while elephants are served leafy branches and hay. To learn more, ask about feeding times at your zoo, or find out if there are any special programs that offer a behind-the-scenes look at the food that is organized and prepared.

LOOK AROUND

If you check out the different exhibits at the zoo, you'll notice that they vary from one animal to another. A mountain gorilla exhibit may have plenty of trees and boulders while a polar bear exhibit will include blocks of ice and a pool. Zoo planners try to re-create the animals' natural habitats to make them feel at home. How many different animal habitats at the zoo can you spot?

ANIMALS

Zoos are home to hundreds—even thousands—of animals from all over the world. Some zoos, such as safari parks, may specialize in specific animals such as African lions and impalas, while others include a mix of creatures.

HAVE FUN

Now that you've completed your tour of the zoo, it's time to put your knowledge to the test by designing a zoo exhibit. First, pick an animal to research. Where does the animal live in the wild? What is its habitat like? Is the climate warm and damp or cold and dry? You'll also want to learn about the animal's shelter and predators. After you've finished gathering your information, grab some paper and markers and begin designing a zoo exhibit for your animal. Include features that will help your animal feel at home and be sure not to include animals that may harm it.

fun fact

The oldest zoo in the world was created in Vienna, Austria, in 1752. Today it is dedicated to species conservation.

Make a BAROMETER

ARE YOU FASCINATED BY WEATHER AND ALL OF THE cool things that happen in nature? Well you should make your own barometer to track the weather where you live!

fun fact

Some parts of the Atacama Desert in Chile haven't had rain in more than 500 years!

SUPPLY LIST

- Ruler
- Tall glass
- Drinking straw
- Bubble gum
- Tape
- Water and blue food coloring

STEPS

1. Tape a clear drinking straw to a ruler. The bottom of the straw should line up with the ½-inch (12–13 mm) mark on the ruler.
2. Stand the ruler up in a tall glass and tape it to the inside of the glass so it stays straight. Fill the glass ¾ full with water.
3. Here's the fun part: Chew on a piece of gum for a while then stick it to the top of the straw.
4. Pour out ¼ of the water so that the water in the straw is higher than the water in the cup.
5. Keep an eye on your barometer. When atmospheric pressure increases, the water level in your straw will rise (which usually means fair weather). When atmospheric pressure decreases, the water level will fall (and can mean clouds or rain are on the way). Record your findings in your meteorologist notebook!

Time: about 10 minutes

KEEP A WEATHER JOURNAL

Recording the daily temperature, rainfall, and barometric changes will help you track patterns in the weather. Try to take a measurement every day and record it in a journal. Set up a chart for each component of your weather station. After a few weeks, you might start to see some patterns, and soon you'll be making predictions—like a regular meteorologist!

Name that INSECT

There are 900,000 known insect species living on the planet, and scientists think there may be millions more we haven't yet named. Here are a few you might find around your town. Can you identify them?

A

With a migration of more than 3,000 miles (4,828 km), these orange-and-black insects make their way to their wintering grounds in southern California and Mexico, sometimes flying 100 miles (161 km) in a day!

B

This uninvited guest to a picnic lives in a colony of up to 10,000. It can smell like rotten coconut when squashed!

C

No wonder its jumping ability is part of its name—this insect can leap 20 times its body length!

fun fact

Carnivorous plants, like the Venus flytrap, eat insects! When the flytrap snaps its jagged trapdoor shut, its digestive enzymes, similar to the ones in our stomach, slowly consume the insect.

D

It is just a myth that these insects crawl in ears, and they definitely don't wear hairpieces! But they do have pincers that they might use in self-defense.

E

With a head that can swivel 180 degrees, this fierce predator can see all—and is quick to catch all.

F

It may look like a blinking fairy on a summer night, but it's actually a beetle!

G

One of the most ancient insects on Earth, these pests know how to get around. They can sprint at 12 feet (3.7 m) per second!

A. Monarch butterfly; **B.** Odorous house ant; **C.** Grasshopper; **D.** Earwig; **E.** Praying mantis; **F.** Firefly; **G.** Cockroach

Plant a BUTTERFLY GARDEN

INVITE BUTTERFLIES TO PICNIC IN YOUR BACKYARD!

All you need to do is create a welcoming habitat and plant the foods they like to eat. Create a butterfly garden in your own yard or work with your local community garden or school to plant one there.

fun fact

Butterflies live on every continent except Antarctica.

BENEFITS OF BUTTERFLIES

Besides being pretty, butterflies are pollinators! Like bees, they travel to flowers seeking nectar and in the process spread pollen from one area to another. That's why "nectar plants" are an important part of your butterfly garden. They help spread the growth of important plants to many other places.

SUPPLY LIST

- Butterfly-friendly plants
- "Host" plants

STEPS

1. Chose a spot for your garden: Butterflies like lots of sun, so make sure you plant your garden in an area that gets at least six hours of direct sunlight.
2. Besides sun, butterflies need protection from wind and rain. Make sure trees and/or shrubs are a part of your butterfly garden.
3. Find out which butterflies you should attract. Certain butterflies like certain types of plants. Look in a field guide or ask a ranger at a local park about which butterfly species are common in your area.
4. Once you know which types of butterflies you're trying to lure, you can narrow in on the best types of plants to buy. Your local nursery can guide you. Start with some "nectar plants." Many butterflies are attracted to coneflower, lilac, and purple verbena. Try to pick plants that bloom at different times of the year so butterflies are always attracted to your garden.
5. Butterflies will also need some "host plants" such as milkweed to lay their eggs on. Your nursery can help you select the best ones.
6. Set up some chairs or a bench to watch your garden! Butterflies are less shy than birds and usually don't mind people being around them.

Time: a full afternoon to plant your garden

CLOSE TO HOME

Regardless of where you live, there is a neighborhood in your town. Neighborhoods are places in or near a city where people live and interact. They include houses, schools, museums, and outdoor areas for people to enjoy. In large cities, several thousand people can live in a neighborhood, but a small town neighborhood may be home to only a few. What are some places in your area that you can explore? That depends on where you live. Here are a few things to look out for.

EXPLORE

LOOK UP

Peregrine falcons are birds of prey that typically nest on high cliff ledges and dive from tall heights to catch and kill other birds. So it seems almost natural that these birds have discovered the perks of city living. Many peregrine falcons have been spotted nesting on the ledges of skyscrapers and other tall buildings, as well as on water towers and bridges. So next time you're around a tall structure, look up! You might spot a falcon.

LOOK DOWN

You may not have to travel to a tropical rain forest to find a strangler fig or climb a mountain to find an alpine phacelia flower. In addition to showcasing native plants, many botanical gardens have special exhibits to display plants that grow in different environments around the world.

Visit the botanical garden in your city. How many unusual plants can you find?

FOR THE DOGS

Most dogs need a lot of exercise, but many city homes don't offer much space for dogs to move around. Fortunately, many cities and nearby towns have dog parks—confined outdoor areas in which dogs can run around and play with other dogs. Some of these parks even have pools of water for dogs to splash around in. Woof! Do you have a dog park where you live?

fun fact

Ohlone Dog Park in Berkeley, California, was the first dog park in the world. It was created in 1979.

HAVE FUN

Have you ever had friends or family members visit from out of town and ask for suggestions about things to do and see? Next time, be ready for them! Make a travel brochure that highlights the best parts of your town. Describe the areas and include photos. Also, draw a map or provide directions to help your visitors get around. Make sure you include great outdoor areas where they can explore nature; they'll really appreciate it!

Make ROCK ART

HUMANS HAVE BEEN CARVING AND DRAWING ON ROCKS for thousands of years. Find rocks in your neighborhood and use them as a canvas to make beautiful art of your own! For inspiration, look online at some Native American rock art or early human rock artwork from around the world.

fun fact

Eight thousand years ago in the Sahara, humans carved full-size images of giraffes into rocks, a reminder that the desert was once a lush landscape with large African wildlife.

SUPPLY LIST

- A few flat rocks (river rocks are nice and smooth)
- Soap and sponge
- Paint, paintbrushes

STEPS

1. Look up some of the animals and designs found at Newspaper Rock State Park in Utah, U.S.A., or in Lascaux Cave in France.
2. Clean your rock with soap and a sponge to make sure it is dirt free.
3. Start painting! Acrylic or outdoor paints will last longest. Tempera paint is less likely to stain hands and clothes, but it isn't all weather.
4. Display your rock in a garden or bring it inside and use it as a doorstop or paperweight.

Time: about 25 minutes

ANCIENT ART

Some of the world's oldest rock art has been found in Lascaux Cave in France. Animals painted on the walls—like horses, bison, mammoth, deer, and wolves—are believed to be about 17,300 years old!

Name that ROCK

Whether you're kicking one down the road or climbing on top of one at the park, rocks are all around you. But what kind of rocks are they? Can you identify the variety of rocks on this page?

A

This is the stuff of hopscotch and tic-tac-toe. It was formed with the skeletons of microorganisms.

B

This volcanic rock forms after lava has cooled quickly, and it is the only rock that floats!

D This rock is so soft it can break up in water.

C This rock formed in a similar way to granite, but you can see large crystals in it.

fun fact

Diamonds are the hardest rocks on Earth. They come in a variety of colors, including yellow, red, and even green.

E Some of the oldest fossils found on Earth are preserved in this soft sedimentary rock.

F The most common volcanic rock on Earth, it formed by cooling quickly, but it has fine grains on the surface.

G A seated Abraham Lincoln and Michelangelo's "David" were both carved out of this white, sedimentary rock.

A. Chalk; **B.** Pumice; **C.** Gabbro; **D.** Mudstone; **E.** Shale; **F.** Basalt; **G.** Marble

LET'S GO TO THE PARK

PARKS ALL AROUND US

There are thousands of parks in the United States and across the globe, most of which are unique in some way. Some parks can be smaller than a city block, while others are as large as some countries. Some parks are known for their geological formations, others have historical significance, and some have diverse plant and animal life. Check out some of these cool parks from around the world.

BANFF NATIONAL PARK

This popular national park is situated among the majestic Canadian Rocky Mountains. It was founded in 1885 and was the first national park to be established in Canada. In addition to the mountains, there are rushing rivers, gigantic glaciers, and lakes so beautifully blue that they look like they can't be real (but they are!). And you can't forget about the plants and animals that call this park home. There are tall evergreen trees that line the landscape and lots of elk, bears, river otters, and even wolves that live in this park.

KAKADU NATIONAL PARK

This national park is located in Australia's National Territory and is also a World Heritage site. Aborigines, the native peoples of Australia, have been living on this land for more than 50,000 years! The park is home to lots of animal species including insects, birds, fish, and the famous saltwater crocodile. There are also ancient cave paintings and rock carvings in different areas of the park that depict what life was like for the prehistoric people who lived there long ago.

SERENGETI NATIONAL PARK

Serengeti National Park in Tanzania is home to tons of wildlife including elephants, giraffes, and lions. But it is probably best known for the yearly migration of thousands of wildebeest, gazelles, and zebras—the largest migration of land mammals in the world! The park is also famous for being one of the best places to watch a sunset.

YELLOWSTONE NATIONAL PARK

Yellowstone National Park, which was established in 1872, is so large that it straddles three U.S. states: Wyoming, Montana, and Idaho. The park is known all over the world for its geysers and hot springs, as well as its diverse wildlife. This includes elk, bison, bighorn sheep, grizzly bears, and trumpeter swans. The park is also home to a once endangered species: the gray wolf.

FIORDLAND NATIONAL PARK

The largest national park in New Zealand, this beautiful area is home to rugged mountains, amazing fjords (inlets of water between cliffs or steep slopes), and many stunning waterfalls. There are also lots of animals that call this park home, including the kakapo, the only flightless parrot in the world.

NATiONAL PARKS

National parks are found all over the world, from Yellowstone in the United States to Fuji-Hakone-Izu in Japan. National parks have been established over the years as a way to preserve and protect our outdoor spaces and the plants and animals that live in them. In 1872, Yellowstone became the first national park in the United States to be recognized by Congress. Since then, almost 60 U.S. national parks have been established. Many other countries have done the same. Explore a few of these parks on the following page, then visit a national park near you!

EXPLORE

LOOK UP

National parks often contain lots of different natural structures. One of the most stunning may be Mount Fuji in Japan's Fuji-Hakone-Izu National Park. Mount Fuji is the highest mountain in Japan and also an active volcano! It is so large that on a clear day you can see it from Japan's capital city, Tokyo, which is 60 miles (100 km) away. In warm months, the grounds are covered in a stunning rainbow of flowers.

LOOK AROUND

Many national parks are known for their unusual rock formations. One of the most famous is the Grand Canyon National Park in Arizona, U.S.A. The park's main attraction is the canyon itself—a giant gorge that was carved out by the Colorado River over millions of years. The canyon is 18 miles (29 km) deep and a staggering 277 miles (446 km) across. That's more than the distance from New York City to Boston!

ANIMALS

Since national parks can have different habitats and different climates, their animal inhabitants will also vary. For example, the dry heat of Desert National Park in India is the ideal home for the monitor lizard, while the marshes and semitropical climate of Florida's Everglades National Park suit the American alligator. Note: Keep your distance from the wild animals you observe, and if possible, stay with a tour guide.

HAVE FUN

Most parks have miles of hiking trails that allow you to get some exercise as you take in the park's landscape. Although these trails are usually marked with signs to help you with direction, some people still get lost. To help remember your way back, stack some small, flat rocks into piles along the trail. Then place a pointed stone on the top of the pile with the sharpest edge facing the direction you took. While returning from your hike, you can look for your rock piles to point you in the right direction.

fun fact

Wrangell-St. Elias Park in Alaska, U.S.A., spans 13.2 million acres (5.34 million ha). That's larger than Switzerland!

Make a KiTE

MAKE THE MOST OF A BREEZY DAY AND GO FLY A KITE.
With a few simple materials you can make your own. Try this basic diamond-shaped design, and once you've had success, start experimenting with different shapes and materials.

fun fact

Benjamin Franklin was a Founding Father of the United States and an author, printer, musician, politician, and inventor. Since childhood, he was very interested in scientific experiments. Once he made a kite and fastened it to his toe to see if it could pull him across water. It worked!

SUPPLY LIST

- 1 13-gallon (50 l) "kitchen-size" plastic trash bag
- 2 wooden dowels: one 24 inches (61 cm) long; the other 20 inches (50 cm) long
- Scissors
- String or fishing line
- Ruler
- Packing tape
- Ribbon
- Permanent markers

STEPS

1. Cut open the trash bag so it is rectangle-shaped.
2. Take your longer dowel and measure 6 inches (15 cm) down and make a mark. Lay the short stick across the long stick at the mark, forming a T. Tie the sticks together.

3. Lay your T on top of the trash bag and cut the plastic around it into a diamond shape, leaving 2 extra inches (5 cm) around the points of the sticks.
4. Cut a 20-inch (50 cm) piece of string. Wrap the string around the top and bottom of the wooden dowels. Tie and make sure it's tight.
5. Fold the edges of the plastic over the dowels and securely tape them down.
6. Tie the end of a large spool of string or fishing line to the middle of the string you just attached.

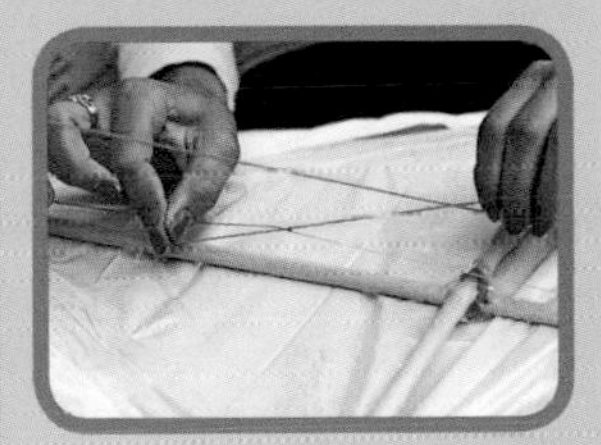

7. Tape some ribbon to the bottom of your diamond to create a tail. Add some bows for beauty! Decorate the plastic with markers.
8. Wait for a breeze; your kite is ready for liftoff!

Time: about 40 minutes

Name that CLOUD

There's nothing like lying down in the grass and looking up at the clouds. Clouds come in all sorts of shapes and sizes. They can be anything you imagine. Do you know the scientific names for different types of clouds? Try to see if you can identify these.

A

These clouds look just like the kind you picture in a cartoon strip—flat on the bottom and fluffy around the edges.

B

These low-lying clouds look like ripples of gray puffballs across the sky.

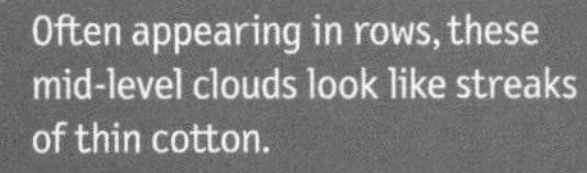

C

Often appearing in rows, these mid-level clouds look like streaks of thin cotton.

D

Known as "thunderheads," these mushroom-shaped clouds mean heavy rainfall or snow is coming.

E

These high-altitude wispy clouds are sometimes called "mare's tails."

fun fact

The makeup of clouds on other planets in our solar system is quite different from ours. While Earth's clouds are made of water (and ice), Venus has clouds made of sulfuric acid and Jupiter and Saturn have clouds made of ammonia!

F

These clouds only form over mountain peaks and sometimes look like flying saucers or a tall hat!

A. Cumulus; **B.** Stratocumulus; **C.** Altocumulus; **D.** Cumulonimbus; **E.** Cirrus; **F.** Altocumulus lenticularis, or "hat cloud"

PARKS in all seasons

SPRING

Horses have been trotting the trails of Colorado's Rocky Mountain since it became a national park in 1915. The park has two stables: Glacier Creek and Moraine Park. Visitors can saddle up and head for the riding trails that span 250 miles (403 km) of the park. On horseback, you'll cover more ground than you would on foot—and see many of the park's springtime blooms, such as the Colorado columbine and the tall chiming bells.

SUMMER

Summer is rainy season in Big Bend—a national park located on the international boundary of Mexico and the United States. The rain increases the water level and flow of the park's famed river, the Rio Grande. This often makes conditions ideal for white-water rafting. With the help of a professional guide, rafters can navigate the Rio Grande as it winds through some of the park's canyons—such as Santa Elena, the Contrabando, and the Boquillas.

Many national parks offer a variety of recreational and sightseeing activities for visitors to enjoy in all seasons. Whether it's skiing and snowboarding in the winter or white-water rafting in the summer, these activities allow people to have fun any time of year.

FALL

Acadia National Park in Maine, U.S.A., covers only 47,000 acres (19,020 ha), making it one of the smallest national parks in the United States. However, with 2.4 million visitors in 2012 alone, the park is also one of the most visited. One of the biggest draws of Acadia is the fall foliage displayed by its deciduous trees. The leaves begin to change color in September and peak in mid-October. The sight is a treat for the park's hikers, mountain bikers, and campers.

WINTER

Sagramatha National Park in Nepal is a protected area in the Himalayan mountain range that is full of rugged snowcapped mountains. One of these mountains is Everest, the tallest in the world. Standing at 29,029 feet (8,848 m) high it reaches above the clouds! As fall turns into winter, temperatures in this park drop below freezing with heavy snowfall. The coldest month is January. This is when temperatures on the mountain can drop to minus 76°F (-60°C). That's really cold!

STATE PARKS

There are more than 6,600 state parks in the United States! State parks are home to many plant and animal species and may have unique features such as volcanoes, glaciers, deserts, and waterfalls.

Niagara Falls, located on the border of New York State and Ontario, Canada, is the oldest state park in the United States. It was established in 1885 as the Niagara Reservation after a group of environmentalists wanted to stop industrialists who were building factories along the water.

EXPLORE

LISTEN UP

Many parks have unusual sights, but Indiana Dunes State Park has some unusual sounds: It's home to "singing" sand. The park's dunes, which may reach heights of almost 200 feet (61 m), produce a booming sound. The sound is made by sand particles, which are all roughly the same size. When wind causes the particles to flow over each other, they hit each other at the same frequency—much like a bow rubbing over a string. This produces sound. Does the sand in your park or beach make a sound? Tune in when the wind blows or listen for a crunching sound as you walk over it.

LOOK DOWN

Fossils have been discovered in many parks, but Dinosaur State Park in Connecticut contains one of the largest dinosaur track sites in North America. About 2,000 tracks have been discovered! The remains of the dinosaurs that created the tracks have not been found, but scientists believe that a *Dilophosaurus,* a medium-size meat-eater that lived about 200 million years ago, was responsible.

ANIMALS

Like national parks, state parks have diverse wildlife. In South Dakota's Custer State Park, you might see bison, elk, and mountain goats, whereas in Kansas's Prairie Dog State Park, you'll find a prairie dog colony and fish such as black bass. Meanwhile, Lewis and Clark State Park in Iowa is home to deer, rabbit, and many different birds. What kinds of animals live in state parks near you?

HAVE FUN

Go on a fossil-finding expedition. First, research where you might find fossils. You can get this information from a paleontology society website or at the visitors center of your local natural history museum. Then head to the park or other public area where digging for fossils is allowed. Many fossils are found in sedimentary rocks, such as limestone or sandstone. Sedimentary rocks are easy to identify because they look like layers. Next, examine the area closely for objects that have shapes and textures different from the rocks around them. If you make a discovery, notify a park ranger or the person or people in charge.

fun fact

The longest dinosaur ever discovered was 125 feet (38 m) long. That's longer than any other animal known to man.

Make a BiRDBATH

HAVE YOU EVER NOTICED BIRDS USE FOUNTAINS IN parks as birdbaths? Why not make a birdbath of your own to invite the birds to your yard? You can make a unique tub for the birds. Then watch as they come by to splish and splash!

fun fact

Some birds—like quail—bathe in the dirt! This prevents their feathers from getting oily. Wrens and sparrows often take a water bath and follow up with a dust bath. Looks like fun!

HOW DO BIRDS EAT WITH NO TEETH?

Birds eat lots of hard seeds and grains, but how do they digest them without chewing? Birds have an organ in their lower stomach called a gizzard. The gizzard's job is to mix and mash the food so it can be digested. It does this by using tiny shells, rocks, and even sand to break the food apart. Where do these materials come from? Birds often pick them up and swallow them while picking up their usual food with their beaks.

SUPPLY LIST

- 3 terra-cotta planters of various sizes
- 1 flower pot saucer that is a few inches larger in circumference than the smallest flower pot
- Acrylic paint
- Heavy-duty outdoor glue

STEPS

1. Gather up some terra-cotta pots and saucers. Try turning one upside down and then stack one right side up on top of it. Then place a large saucer on top of the highest pot, or turn three different-size pots upside down and stack them in descending order. Then place a large saucer on top.
2. Once you have decided on a shape for your birdbath, it's time to start painting! Spray paint or any other outdoor paint will work. Ask an adult for help. Choose a variety of colors. Try using a small paintbrush to add some designs to make your birdbath unique!
3. Once the pots and saucers are dry, have an adult use outdoor permanent glue to attach the pieces and form the design you choose.
4. Once the glue is dry, fill up your birdbath with water! Remember the water in the shallow saucer will evaporate quickly. Keep it filled so the birds can swoop in to freshen up!

Time: an hour or more, plus drying time

Name that OUTDOOR SPORT

It is impossible to suffer from the doldrums when you're in the outdoors. Whether you're hanging out in your neighborhood park or on a national park road trip, the options are limitless for things to do. Can you identify these outdoor activities?

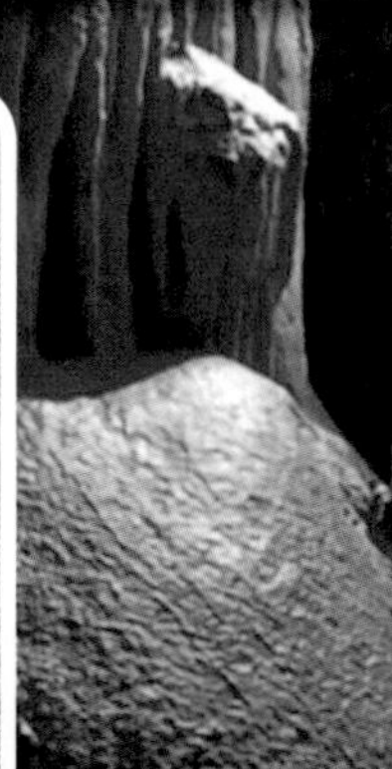

A

A fun-to-say synonym for this underground sport is spelunking.

B

This sport can take you anywhere, as long as you have some traction.

C

You don't have to head over to the O.K. Corral to experience this outdoor sport—but chaps wouldn't hurt.

D

When you're ready to start a pitch, make sure to shout "on belay!"

fun fact

Map reading can be a sport! Orienteering combines accurate map-and-compass reading skills with running. Individuals and teams compete to find markers along trails. The person (or team) that completes the course the fastest wins!

E

The name of the boat used for this type of sport is a palindrome! (It is spelled the same way forward and backward.)

F

Those aren't tennis rackets on your feet, but they do "serve" a purpose for keeping you from sinking in powdery snow.

A. Caving; **B.** Hiking; **C.** Horseback riding; **D.** Rock climbing; **E.** Kayaking; **F.** Snowshoeing

Make a SOLAR OVEN

YOU DON'T NEED A CAMPFIRE TO COOK IN THE GREAT outdoors—you can have a cookout by the heat of the sun! Using a pizza box and aluminum foil, you can make your own solar oven to bake mini pizzas—and even s'mores!

fun fact

If it's hot enough outside, you may be able to fry an egg on the sidewalk! How hot of a day does it have to be? As a rule of thumb, if the sidewalk is so hot you can't even walk on it barefoot, it might be hot enough to slowly cook an egg.

HOW DOES A SOLAR OVEN WORK?

The aluminum foil helps reflect the sunlight into the box. The black construction paper helps absorb the heat. The plastic wrap layers create insulation to keep the heat in the box. If all is working well, your solar oven will heat up to about 200°F (93°C). Your oven inside your house gets much hotter, but your pizza box oven should warm food up—and melt chocolate for a tasty s'more.

SUPPLY LIST

- Cardboard pizza box
- Aluminum foil
- Clear plastic wrap
- Black construction paper
- Tape
- Scissors
- Ruler or stick

STEPS

1. Using scissors, cut three sides of a square in the lid of a pizza box to create a flap. Cut a large enough square so there is about 2 inches (5 cm) of space left on all four sides of the box.

2. Cover the inner side of the flap with foil, with the shiniest side facing out. Tape the foil to the cardboard flap.
3. Open the box and cover the inside with foil—again with the shiniest side facing out and taping it down to the cardboard. Line the bottom of the box with black construction paper.

4. With the box open, tape a layer of plastic wrap over the open flap hole, making sure the wrap is pulled tightly and all sides are taped down. Close the lid and add a second layer of wrap over the flap hole, again pulling to make sure it is taut and firmly taped down.

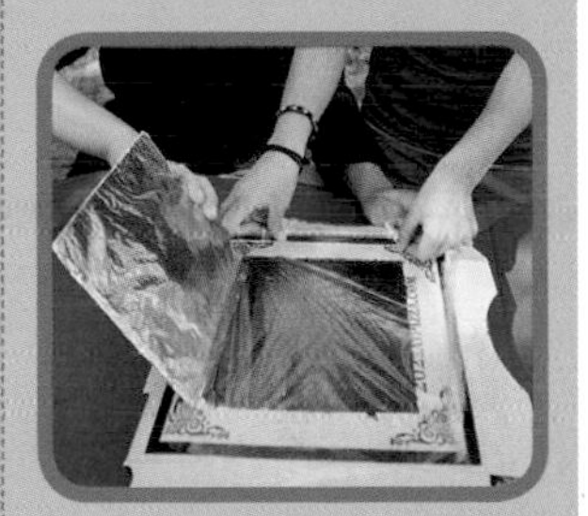

5. Find a nice, sunny spot for your oven. Place your food—an English muffin with tomato sauce and shredded cheese might be a good food to try first—on the black paper and close the lid. Prop the flap open with a ruler or long stick.
6. Wait for your food to heat up (it will probably take about half an hour) and enjoy!

Time: 30 minutes, plus cooking time

LOCAL PARKS

Local parks have been around for about 1,000 years, but their original purpose was different from what they're used for today. Many early parks in England were established to hold animals such as deer. But in the late 1700s to early 1800s that began to change. Many cities were being built and people longed to have public spaces where they could go to escape the hustle and bustle of urban living. So they set aside natural areas where they could relax and enjoy the outdoors. These areas became parks.

EXPLORE

LOOK DOWN

If you see a single ant circling a picnic scrap, you can be sure that other ants will soon follow. Why? Many ant species live together in large groups called colonies. When one member of a colony comes across a food source, it communicates the information to the other members by using chemical scents. Next time you observe an ant at your picnic site, time how long it takes for the other ants to take note.

ANIMALS

Animals in local parks may vary from region to region. Some critters that are usually common in parks include tree squirrels, pigeons, and many insects such as grasshoppers, bees, and butterflies.

LOOK AROUND

It's against the law to litter in most parks around the world. Litter ruins a park's appearance and can harm wildlife. If you notice garbage is building up in your park, organize a clean-up party. Make sure you wear gloves to protect yourself and place the litter in appropriate trash and recycle bins. The animals will thank you!

HAVE FUN

Frisbee is a popular sport played in many parks. Polish your Frisbee-throwing skills with these tips: First, grasp the Frisbee by the rim. Your thumb should be on top of the Frisbee and your index finger along the outer edge. Next, stand with your knees slightly bent. If you are right-handed, your right foot should be up front, and if you are left-handed, your left foot should be up front. Cross your arm over your chest, then swing the Frisbee forward and release.

fun fact

Mill Ends Park in Portland, Oregon, U.S.A., may be the world's tiniest park. It measures only two feet (61 cm) across! It was dedicated on St. Patrick's Day in 1948 to a "colony of leprechauns."

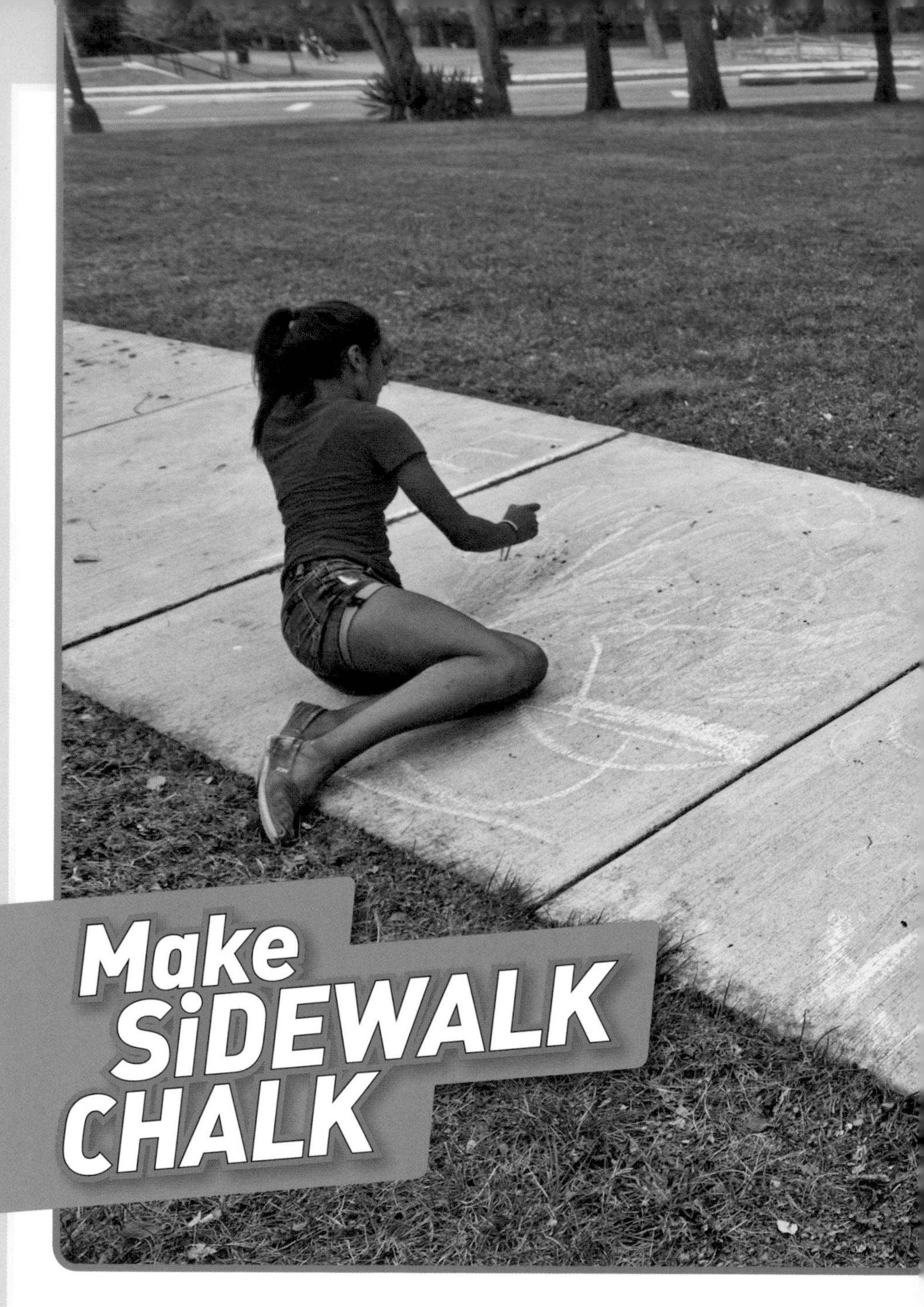

Make SiDEWALK CHALK

JAZZ UP YOUR SIDEWALK BY MAKING YOUR OWN sidewalk chalk—with colors of your choosing! Make up a few batches of this chalk and head outside to create some cool art!

fun fact

In India hopscotch is called *kith-kith* and in Brazil it's called *amarelinha.*

SUPPLY LIST

- Tempera paint (various colors)
- Plaster of Paris (found at craft or hardware stores)
- Water
- Cardboard tubes (such as wrapping paper or paper towel tubes)
- Wax paper
- Masking tape
- Plastic sandwich bags
- Scissors
- Silicone cupcake molds (optional)

STEPS

1. Cut a paper towel tube in half, or cut a wrapping paper tube into 5-inch (13 cm) segments. Line the insides of the tube with wax paper. Seal one end of each tube with masking tape. (You can also fill up fun-shaped silicone cupcake holders instead of the tubes. Just know you won't be able to bake with them again!)

2. Mix 2 to 4 tablespoons (2–3½ UK tbsp) tempera paint with 1 cup (235 mL) water in a disposable container. Slowly stir 1½ cups (350 mL) plaster of Paris until thoroughly combined. Spoon the mix into a sandwich bag and cut off one end, like you would for piping frosting. Squeeze the mixture into the cardboard tube.
3. Tap the bottom of the tubes to break up bubbles and prop the tubes up for drying.

4. The chalk will take about 24 hours to dry. When ready, peel back the cardboard and head outside to create some sidewalk art!

Time: 30 minutes, plus overnight to dry

HISTORY OF HOPSCOTCH

It is thought that the game may have started in China or Greece. In Roman times, hopscotch courts were used to help exercise Roman soldiers and improve their footwork. Today, hopscotch is a popular sport all over the world. Its rules may vary, but no matter where you play, it sure is fun!

Name that BiRD

Whether you're in your yard, hiking in the woods, or at a park, you don't have to go far to spot some wildlife—you just need to look up. Can you identify these common birds?

A

The males of this sharp-crested species are an eye-catching streak of red flying overhead.

B

These smart, large birds with a distinct caw are black from beak to legs.

C

These bright-orange, lightning-fast birds are quick to beat out the competition at feeders and flowers.

D

Found on telephone wires and on the ground looking for seeds, their sad calls are what give these birds their name.

fun fact

Hummingbirds get 90 percent of their food from flowers' nectar. Relative to their size, hummingbirds eat 77 times as much food per day as humans do!

E

Found in city parks around the world, these birds are often seen fearlessly walking around pecking crumbs.

F

You may hear these birds before you see them. They poke thousands of holes in trees every year with their strong beaks then place acorns inside.

G

With their distinct, floppy head plume, these birds are often seen searching for food on the ground and only fly for a few seconds at a time.

A. Northern cardinal; **B.** American crow; **C.** Rufous hummingbird; **D.** Mourning dove; **E.** Rock pigeon; **F.** Acorn woodpecker; **G.** California quail

GET OUTSIDE with National Geographic EXPLORERS

Mbunya Francis Nkemnyi, Conservationist

Mbunya Francis Nkemnyi was born in the African country of Cameroon. He originally wanted to be a doctor, but after going on a college class trip to Cameroon's Korup National Park, it became clear to him that he had a passion for plant and animal conservation. He talked with many conservationists at the park and was inspired to become one himself. Today, he spends much of his time collecting data and performing field surveys as part of a camping station team. One of his favorite things about being in the field is the teamwork and connectedness that comes from sharing a day with his fellow conservationists.

www.nationalgeographic.com/explorers/bios/mbunya-francis-nkemnyi

Stephen Sillett, Forest Scientist

As a kid, Stephen Sillett spent lots of time outdoors in the forests of the United States' Appalachian Mountains. He frequently watched birds, caught reptiles and amphibians, and climbed trees in the woods. Today he still spends time with trees. His days usually involve scaling trees to map their structures, installing equipment, and collecting samples. While working with a National Geographic Society team, Stephen was able to climb and install equipment to document a 3,200-year-old giant sequoia! He considers this his favorite experience.

www.nationalgeographic.com/explorers/bios/stephen-sillett

Becca Skinner, Photographer

Though she loves exploring and taking pictures purely for enjoyment, Becca Skinner's main goal is to provide a voice to people who are often not heard. Her largest projects have included photographing the aftermaths of natural disasters. Becca believes that the recovery and rebuilding process is just as important as the disaster itself, and she hopes to help share the stories of communities affected by nature. Her favorite experience in the field was flying a kite among rice paddies with local villagers in Sumatra, an island in western Indonesia. Sounds like a great outdoor adventure!

www.nationalgeographic.com/explorers/bios/becca-skinner

Tshewang Wangchuk, Conservationist

Growing up in Bhutan, a country in South Asia, Tshewang Wangchuk was always close to nature—rivers and forests, wildlife, and especially mountains. Always being surrounded by mountains, Tshewang is familiar with the important role they play in the natural world and the special role they play in the lives of the majestic snow leopard. Tshewang devotes himself to studying snow leopards in their mountain habitat in the hopes of saving these endangered animals. Two of Tshewang's favorite things about being in the mountains are enjoying the beauty of the landscape and talking with local people he comes across as he does his fieldwork.

www.nationalgeographic.com/explorers/bios/tshewang-wangchuk

THE CHILDREN & NATURE NETWORK

In today's world, people tend to spend more time using technology such as smartphones and tablets and less time exploring the great outdoors.

In 2005, author Richard Louv wrote a book called *Last Child in the Woods*, in which he came up with the term "nature-deficit disorder" to describe our society's lack of interaction with nature. To try to change this trend, Louv co-founded the Children & Nature Network (C&NN). This organization brings children together with nature through new ideas, resources, and community partnerships.

Check out the C&NN website (www.childrenandnature.org) to discover exciting outdoor activities you and your family can try, from water games to snow sports and mountain trails to after-dark adventures. Become an animal detective, spend a day sledding, or get tips on backyard camping. You can also explore nature through C&NN's enormous list of recommended research, news, and original writing.

Through C&NN, you and your family can help build the new nature movement—at home and in your community. C&NN gives you access to tool kits and other information to create your own events and celebrations. You can join—or create!—a family nature club (multiple families coming together for outdoor adventures) and download an online tool kit to help get you started. If activism is more your style, C&NN's website also gives you the tools to start up your own grassroots leadership campaign to connect people to nature, conserve the environment, and even create new natural habitats in your backyard or city. C&NN helps you search for local nature events or join in on national ones, such as Serve Outside September (SOS) or Let's GO! (Outside), celebrations that focus both on playing in nature and protecting it. At the C&NN website you can download a tool kit and badge to join in on these events and help support natural areas, all while having a blast. Be sure to also check out the contributions of other kids across the country at C&NN Connect, a great place for kids, families, and teachers to post photographs and stories, and to hear about what fellow outdoor adventurers are up to!

LET'S MOVE OUTSIDE

On February 9, 2010, First Lady Michelle Obama launched the *Let's Move!* initiative, dedicated to solving childhood obesity so that kids can grow up to be healthy, happy, and active.

As part of the *Let's Move!* initiative, Let's Move Outside was created to get kids—and adults!—to increase their physical activity by exploring our great outdoors. Let's Move Outside makes it easier to explore nature by giving you fun seasonal ideas for outdoor activities. Head to the Let's Move Outside website (www.letsmove.gov/lets-move-outside) for guides to finding local playgrounds, nearby parks and forests, and outdoor nature events in your neighborhood. Are you into biking? Do you love water sports? Want to explore natural habitats? Let's Move Outside will help you locate nearby hiking trails, bike paths, public pools, and much more. You can also find ideas for healthy snacks to bring along on your adventures, including nutritious, delicious recipes from White House chefs! For rainy days, Let's Move Outside even has links to interactive museum and garden exhibits. By getting outside and into nature, you will improve your physical health, crank up your creativity, and have tons of fun!

If you're looking for even more ways to stay active, *Let's Move!* and Let's Move Outside also have challenges you can issue to yourself and your family. Tackle a recipe challenge issued by the First Lady, or see which of your family members can achieve the Presidential Active Lifestyle Award first. You can even take up the task of planting a garden in your home, school, or community! *Let's Move!* helps you start and keep track of all these goals with fun calendars and logs, as well as tips and tricks for healthy lifestyles. The website is chock-full of activities to do and games to play with your family and ideas for bringing your healthy habits into your school and community. Before you know it, you'll be getting outside and improving your fitness ... and having lots of fun while doing it!

BANCROFT

Alabama

DeSoto
2.2-mile canyon drive; 15 waterfalls; Hiking, swimming, mountain biking; Lodge

Cheaha
Mountain vistas; Hiking, biking, swimming, fishing

Joe Wheeler
Lake; Golfing, tennis, biking, swimming, fishing; Convention/meeting facility

Gulf
Gulf of Mexico beach; Golfing, swimming, tennis

Alaska

Chugach
Hiking, backpacking, mountaineering, mountain biking, rock and ice climbing, horseback riding, fishing; Skiing, snowmobiling; White-water rafting, ATVing; Historic railroad section house

Denali
Mount McKinley viewpoints; Backcountry hiking, white-water kayaking, fishing

Wood-Tikchik
Wilderness camping; Hiking, river running/float trips, fishing

Totem Bight
Interpretive trail; Native Alaskan totem art and architecture

Arizona

Slide Rock
Red-rock canyon; Natural water slide; Apple orchard; Nature walks; Trout fishing, hiking, bird-watching

Red Rock
Nature preserve; Environmental center; Hiking; Wildlife viewing, bird-watching

Tonto Natural Bridge
Natural rock bridge; Nature trails; Swimming, wading; Historic building

Kartchner Caverns
Cavern tours, camping, hiking

Arkansas

Petit Jean
Native American bluff shelters; Mountaintop panoramas; Cedar Falls; Hiking, swimming, boating, fishing

Devil's Den
Geological formations; Mountain stream; Interpretive trails; Backpacking, biking, horseback riding

Village Creek
Unusual geology; Hiking, swimming, fishing, biking, horseback riding

Crater of Diamonds
Diamond hunting

Lake Chicot
Scenic lake; Bird-watching, fishing; Barge tours

California

Anza-Borrego Desert
Desert flora and fauna; Historic trails; Native American rock art; Hiking

Humboldt Redwoods
Old-growth redwoods; Hiking, biking, horseback riding, swimming, canoeing; Summer interpretive programs

Ahjumawi Lava Springs
Undeveloped, access by boat only; Primitive camping, hiking, boating, fishing, bird-watching

Mount Tamalpais
Mountain wilderness; Panoramic views; Spring wildflowers; Mountain Theatre; Hiking, horseback riding

Pfeiffer Big Sur
Redwood groves; Big Sur River; Hiking, swimming; Summer interpretive programs

Ano Nuevo
Breeding ground of northern elephant seals; Rocky beaches; Spring wildflowers; Hiking, sunbathing, picnicking

Colorado

Mueller
Panoramic views of the Rockies; Hiking, mountain biking, horseback riding; Wildlife viewing; Cross-country skiing

Roxborough
Red-rock formations; Unusual mix of wildlife and plant life; Hiking

Golden Gate Canyon
Hiking, mountain biking, horseback riding

Eldorado Canyon
Wild canyon; Rock climbing, hiking, mountain biking

Lory
Hiking, mountain biking, horseback riding; Wildlife viewing; Backcountry camping

Connecticut

Housatonic Meadows
Fly-fishing, hiking, canoeing

Talcott Mountain
Heublein Tower; Hiking

Dinosaur
North America's largest enclosed dinosaur trackway; Footprint casting; Nature trails

Sleeping Giant
Hiking, cross-country skiing

Bluff Point
Bird-watching; Hiking; Wetlands and beach

Delaware

Cape Henlopen
Wild maritime landscape;

Bountiful wildlife; Dune trail; Bird-watching; Hiking, biking, surf fishing

Trap Pond
Bald cypress trees; Nature center; Hiking, biking, canoeing, fishing

Fort Delaware
Historic fort; Heronry

White Clay Creek
Bird-watching; White-tailed deer; Hiking, biking, fishing; Disk golf

Florida

John Pennekamp Coral Reef
Living coral reef; Glass-bottom boat tours; Scuba/snorkeling tours; Nature and canoe trails; Boat rentals; Aquarium

Myakka River
Boat and tram tours; Hiking, bird-watching, fishing, biking

Wekiwa Springs
Natural springs; Swimming, canoeing, hiking

Paynes Prairie
Hiking, fishing

St. Joseph Peninsula
Beaches; Nature trails, boardwalk; Bird-watching

Georgia

Stephen C. Foster
Okefenokee Swamp tours; Boardwalk nature trail; Boating, fishing

Tallulah Gorge
Wild gorge; Rim trail overlooks; Lake swimming, tennis

Fort Mountain
Mountain wilderness; Hiking, swimming, fishing

Cloudland Canyon
Hiking trails; Tennis courts, disk golf

Providence Canyon
Hiking

Hawaii

Na Pali Coast
Sea cliffs, river valleys, waterfalls; Archaeological sites

Waimea Canyon and Kokee
Spectacular gorge; Rain forest; Dramatic views; Hiking

Kealakekua Bay
Site of early foreign contact; Temple ruins; Captain Cook monument; Snorkeling

Iao Valley
Historic site; Lush valley; Rock spire

Iolani Palace
Royal residence and grounds

Idaho

Ponderosa
Old-growth forest; High cliffs; Lake; Boating, fishing, biking, hiking, cross-country skiing

Harriman
Historic buildings; Wildlife viewing; Hiking, mountain biking, horseback riding, cross country skiing, snowshoeing, fishing

Bruneau Dunes
Dune field; Lake, marsh, and desert; Swimming, hiking, fishing; Observatory; Wildlife museum

Old Mission
1850 church

Heyburn
Canoeing, hiking, mountain biking, fishing

Illinois

Giant City
Stone fort; Sandstone formations; Observation platform; Historic lodge; Rare plants; Horseback riding, hiking, fishing

Fort Massac
Ohio River; Re-created fort; Museum; Boating, fishing

Starved Rock
Canyons; Historic lodge; Horseback riding, fishing, boating, hiking

Mississippi Palisades
Limestone cliffs; Boating, hiking, fishing; Bird-watching; Rock climbing

Ferne Clyffe
Waterfalls; Caves; Hiking, fishing

Indiana

Brown County
Scenic views; Covered bridge; Swimming pool; Historic inn; Nature center; Trail rides; Hiking, mountain biking, fishing, cross-country skiing

Spring Mill
Pioneer village; Caves; Astronaut memorial; Nature preserve; Operating gristmill; Hiking, fishing, swimming, mountain biking

Falls of the Ohio
Fossil beds and cliffs; Dam; Bird-watching; kayaking, fishing, hiking; Interpretive center

Indiana Dunes
Nature center; Swimming beach; Sand dunes; Marshes; Hiking, cross-country skiing

Iowa

Backbone
Hiking, swimming, boating, fishing, rock climbing, winter sports

Ledges
Hiking, bird-watching

Maquoketa Caves
Karst topography; Cave exploration; Hiking

Stone
Loess Hills; Hiking, biking, horseback riding

Kansas

Lake Scott
Pueblo ruins; Hiking, swimming, fishing

Prairie Dog
Fishing; Prairie dog town

Clinton
Swimming, boating, fishing, biking; Mountain bike skills course

Elk City
Hiking, fishing, boating, swimming

Kentucky

Cumberland Falls
Hiking, swimming, fishing, horseback riding; Waterfalls; Moonbow; White-water rafting

Natural Bridge
Sandstone arch; Skylift; Hiking; Nature center; Lodge; Lake, swimming pool

Carter Caves
20 caverns; Natural bridges; Hiking, golfing, tennis, swimming, horseback riding, fishing; Fieldstone lodge

John James Audubon
Art museum; Nature center; Hiking, golfing, bird-watching, paddleboats

Louisiana

Lake Fausse Pointe
Atchafalaya Swamp; Canoeing trails; Hiking; Boat rentals; Conference center

Chicot
Hiking, fishing; Boat and canoe rentals

Poverty Point
Museum; Seasonal tram tours; Self-guided trail

Lake Bistineau
Boating, fishing, hiking, biking

Maine

Baxter
New England's largest state park; Maine's highest mountain; Wildlife viewing; Hiking, boating, fishing

Cobscook Bay
Walking trails; Clamming

Lily Bay
New England's largest lake; Fishing, boating, wildlife viewing

Grafton Notch
Waterfalls; Hiking

Rangeley Lake
Boating, swimming, fishing

Maryland

Assateague
Nature center; Wild horses; Bird-watching; Swimming, boating, fishing

Gunpowder Falls
Scenic river valley; Hiking, biking, swimming, boating

Patapsco Valley
Scenic river valley; Hiking, biking, canoeing, fishing

Swallow Falls
Camping; Hiking; Picnic area

Massachusetts

Walden Pond
National historic landmark; Walking, boating, fishing

Mount Greylock
Hiking, skiing, backpacking

Wachusett Mountain
Scenic views; Hiking, skiing

Pilgrim Memorial
Plymouth Rock

Skinner
Historic inn

Michigan

Mackinac Island
Historic hotel; Carriage rides; Arch Rock; Interpreters; Biking, hiking; National historic landmark

Porcupine Mountains
Waterfalls; Lake of the Clouds; Cross-country and downhill skiing; Fishing, hiking

Fort Wilkins
Lake Superior shore; Costumed interpreters; Historic lighthouse; Fishing, hiking

P.J. Hoffmaster
Sand dunes; Nature center; Swimming beach; Hiking

Hartwick Pines
Pine forest; Logging camp museum; Fishing, hiking, cross-country skiing

Minnesota

Itasca
Mississippi Headwaters; Virgin pine wilderness; Naturalist-led boat tours; Historic lodge; Fishing, biking, swimming; Snowmobiling, cross-country skiing, snowshoeing

Forestville/Mystery Cave
Largest cave in Minnesota; Historic village with interpreters; Spring-fed trout streams; Horseback riding, cross-country skiing

Tettegouche
Palisades; 60-foot waterfall; Hiking, rock climbing, fishing

Soudan Underground Mine
Red-rock formations; Unusual mix of wildlife and plant life; Hiking

Blue Mounds
"Blue" cliff; Tallgrass prairie; Bison herd; Swimming, bird-watching, snowmobiling, rock climbing

Mississippi

Tishomingo
Native American artifacts; Float trips; Hiking, swimming, fishing

Winterville Mounds
Prehistoric Native American mounds; Museum

Natchez
Deep South scenery; Lake; Fishing; Nature trail; Picnic area

Percy Quin
Deep South scenery; Lake; Watersports; Fishing, golfing, swimming, tennis; Nature trail; Conservation center

Missouri

Prairie
Prairie ecosystems; Wildlife; Hiking

Ha Ha Tonka
Castle ruins; Hiking; Karst topography

Montauk
Fishing, hiking

Meramec
Cave tours; Hiking, canoeing, swimming

Montana

Flathead Lake
West's largest natural freshwater lake; Hiking; Abundant wildlife; Boating, swimming, fishing

Bannack
Gold rush ghost town

Chief Plenty Coups
Historic buildings

Makoshika
Scenic badlands; Fossils; Hiking

Nebraska

Fort Robinson
Red Cloud Agency; Bison herd and bighorn sheep; Hiking,

mountain biking, horseback riding, bird-watching, fishing

Lake McConaughy
Swimming, fishing, boating, windsurfing

Arbor Lodge
Historic mansion

Nevada

Lake Tahoe Nevada
Lakeside beaches; Mountain backcountry; Fishing, hiking, mountain biking, cross-country skiing

Valley of Fire
Colorful rock formations; Prehistoric rock art; Petrified wood; Hiking

Cathedral Gorge
Slot canyons; Horseback riding, hiking, biking

Berlin-Ichthyosaur
Marine fossils; Ghost town; Old mine; Seasonal tours

New Hampshire

Franconia Notch
Covered bridges; Waterfalls; Aerial tramway; Hiking, biking, skiing, snowmobiling, fishing

Mount Washington
Highest mountain in New England; Weather observatory; Historic hotel

Robert Frost Farm
National historic landmark; Nature-poetry trail

Odiorne Point
Seacoast Science Center; Remnants of Army fort; Walking and biking trails

New Jersey

Island Beach
Barrier island; Surf fishing; Bird-watching; Swimming, canoeing, kayaking

High Point
Veterans memorial; Appalachian Trail; Bird-watching; Hiking, swimming, fishing, boating, cross-country skiing

Ringwood
Botanical gardens; Historic manors; Hiking, boating, fishing

Allaire
19th-century ironmaking village; Narrow-gauge railroad; Hiking, canoeing, fishing

New Mexico

Sugarite Canyon
1,200-foot-deep canyon; Wildflowers; Boating, hiking, fishing; Cross-country skiing, ice-skating

Clayton Lake
Dinosaur tracks; Rock garden; Fishing, bird-watching, boating

Heron Lake and El Vado Lake
Two scenic lakes; Hiking; Swimming, sailing, boating, windsurfing, fishing, jet skiing; Bird-watching, biking, snowshoeing, cross-country skiing

Oliver Lee Memorial
Desert canyon oasis; Hiking; Bird-watching; Nature trail

New York

Niagara
Boat tour; Discovery center

Taughannock Falls
Highest vertical single-drop falls east of the Rockies; Rim and gorge trails; Summer concerts; Swimming, boating, fishing, cross-country skiing

Letchworth
Bird conservation area; Museum; Historic inn; White-water rafting; Hot-air balloon rides; Hiking, swimming, horseback riding, cross-country skiing, fishing

Allegany
2,200-foot peaks; Hiking, boating, biking, cross-country skiing, horseback riding, snowmobiling

Connetquot
Gristmill and tavern; Trout hatchery; Stocked streams; hiking, fly-fishing

North Carolina

Hanging Rock
300-foot cliffs; Waterfalls; Hiking, rock climbing, boating, fishing, swimming; National historic landmark

Stone Mountain
600-foot granite dome; Hiking; Waterfalls; Rock climbing, trout fishing; Historic structures

Hammocks Beach
Barrier island; Canoe trail; Swimming, shelling, fishing

Fort Macon
Civil War–era fort; Ocean swimming, fishing

North Dakota

Cross Ranch
River-bottom ecology; Hiking

Fort Abraham Lincoln
Native American village; Custer home; Horseback riding, fishing

Lake Metigoshe
Swimming, boating, kayaking; Hiking, cross-country skiing, snowmobiling

Icelandic
Prairie natural area; Pioneer heritage museum; Cross-country skiing

Ohio

Hocking Hills
Waterfalls, caves, hollows; Hiking, swimming, biking, fishing

Hueston Woods
Nature preserve, nature center; Interpretive programs; Pioneer farm museum; Fossils; Hiking, swimming, fishing, boating, golfing, miniature golfing

Kelleys Island
Glacial grooves; Boating, fishing, hiking, swimming beach; Nature preserve; Ferry

Maumee Bay
Nature Center; Wetlands, marshes; Boating, golfing, sledding

Oklahoma

Beavers Bend
Rugged Ouachita Mountains terrain; Mountain Fork River; Broken Bow Reservoir; Nature center; Hiking, nature trails

Quartz Mountain
Rugged granite hills; Lake Altus-Lugert; Nature center; Diverse flora and fauna; Hiking, bird-watching

Black Mesa
Highest point in Oklahoma; Flora, fauna, geology

Osage Hills
Rolling, wooded hills; Scenic creek, bluffs; Hiking

Oregon

Fort Stevens
Military museum; Historic artillery emplacements; *Peter Iredale* shipwreck; Hiking, biking; Beach

Silver Falls
Waterfalls; Historic lodge; Wildflowers; Hiking, biking, horseback riding; Wildlife viewing

Sunset Bay
Rocky coastline; Sandy beach; Seal and sea lion colonies; Historic garden; Hiking, tide pooling, whale-watching

Farewell Bend
Oregon Trail history; Snake River fishing; Camping

Pennsylvania

Ohiopyle
Wild river gorge; Ferncliff Peninsula Natural Area; White-water rafting; Hiking, biking, fishing, snowmobiling, horseback riding, cross-country skiing; Rock climbing

Presque Isle
Coastal wilderness; Bird-watching; Boat tours; Swimming, boating, hiking, bicycling, inline skating, ice skating, cross-country skiing, fishing

Cook Forest
Sawmill craft center and theater; Canoeing, tubing, hiking, swimming, cross-country skiing, fishing

Ricketts Glen
Glens; Waterfalls; Giant trees; Lake; Fishing, boating, swimming, hiking, cross-country skiing

Rhode Island

Fort Adams
Historic fort; Yachting museum; Sailing center; Accessible by water taxi

Beavertail
Lighthouse museum; Scenic overlooks; Biking, fishing

Colt
Historic farm; Open-air chapel and ornamental gardens; Biking and horseback-riding trails

Goddard Memorial
Hiking and horseback-riding trails; Beach; Performing arts center; Golfing, boating

South Carolina

Mountain Bridge
Waterfall; Mountain vistas; Hiking, fishing

Devils Fork
Wilderness area; Boat rentals; Lake swimming, fishing, hiking

Huntington Beach
Beach; Marsh boardwalk; Nature trail; Historic house

Hunting Island
Beach; Historic lighthouse; Nature center; Fishing

South Dakota

Custer
Needles Highway; Bison herd; Rock climbing, mountain biking, fishing, horseback riding, hiking

Fort Sisseton
Visitors centers; Re-created barracks

Newton Hills
Hiking, swimming, fishing, cross-country skiing

Tennessee

Fall Creek Falls
Waterfalls; Hiking; Lake; Nature center; Scenic drive; Resort lodge; Golfing, tennis, swimming, horseback riding, biking

Roan Mountain
Natural rhododendron garden; 6,285-foot peak; Hiking, swimming, camping

Pickett
Natural bridges and overhangs; Hiking, fishing; Lake swimming

Reelfoot Lake
Boat cruises; Bald eagle tours; National wildlife refuge; Wildlife drives; Nature centers; Hiking, fishing

Texas

Big Bend Ranch
Rugged wilderness; Desert wildlife; Barton Warnock Environmental Education Center; Rafting, hiking, backpacking, mountain biking

Enchanted Rock
Pink granite formations; Rock climbing

Brazos Bend
Excellent wildlife viewing; Hiking, biking

Caddo Lake
Nature and hiking trails; Picturesque lake; Canoeing; Recreation hall

Utah

Antelope Island
Buffalo ranch; Scenic loop drive; Saltwater bathing; Boating, bird-watching, hiking, biking, horseback riding; Wildlife viewing

Coral Pink Sand Dunes
Hiking, biking, horseback riding, photography

Dead Horse Point
Interpretive museum; Hiking

Goblin Valley
Hiking; Interactive displays

Kodachrome Basin
Unusual geology; Hiking; Photography

Vermont

Island Complex (Burton, Knight, and Woods)
Remote islands; Hiking and nature trails; Fishing

Smugglers Notch
Mountain pass; Rock formations; Hiking

Button Bay
Fossils; Nature center; Swimming pool, boating, fishing

Mount Philo
Mountain and lake views; Hiking

Virginia

Grayson Highlands
Alpine scenery; Access to Appalachian Trail and Mount Rogers National Recreation Area; Horse camping; Hiking, fishing, mountain biking, cross-country skiing

Douthat
Spectacular mountain setting; Nature programs; Hiking, fishing, boating, swimming

False Cape
Beautiful barrier spit; Hiking, biking, swimming, fishing

First Landing
Cypress swamp; Varied ecosystems; Hiking, biking, boating

Westmoreland
Fossil-filled cliffs; Hiking, swimming, boating, bird-watching; Picnic area

Washington

Deception Pass
Beaches; Forest and wetlands; Interpretive center; Tide pooling; Wildlife viewing, hiking, swimming, boating, fishing

Moran
Mount Constitution; Hiking, wildlife viewing; Boating, swimming, fishing

Cape Disappointment
Lewis and Clark Interpretive Center; Historic lighthouses; Overlook of Columbia River mouth; Benson Beach; Hiking, biking, surf fishing, clamming

Riverside
Spokane House Interpretive Center; Riverside trails; Wetlands; Off-road vehicle park

West Virginia

Pipestem Resort
Bluestone River Gorge; Mountain scenery; Nature center; Horse rentals and trails; Hiking, tennis, swimming, golfing, boating, mountain biking

Blackwater Falls
Blackwater River Canyon; Hiking, cross-country skiing, fishing, mountain biking; Petting zoo

Canaan Valley Resort
Mountain-ringed valley; Interpretive programs; Skiing, ice-skating, hiking, swimming, golfing

Watoga
Hiking, fishing, cross-country skiing

Wisconsin

Devil's Lake
500-foot bluffs; Native American mounds; Nature center; Rock climbing, hiking, fishing, swimming beaches

Peninsula
Green Bay views; Cliffs and caves; Eagle Bluff lighthouse; Summer theater; Beach; Golfing, hiking, biking; Nature center

Rock Island
Historic house; Beach; Hiking

Copper Falls
Ancient lava flows; Waterfalls; Canyons; Hiking, bird-watching, fishing

Wyoming

Sinks Canyon
Scenic canyon with disappearing river; Hiking, wildlife viewing, fishing

Guernsey
Historic buildings; Oregon National Historic Trail; Hiking, swimming, boating

Trail End
Restored 1913 mansion; Carriage house; Landscaped grounds; Picnic area

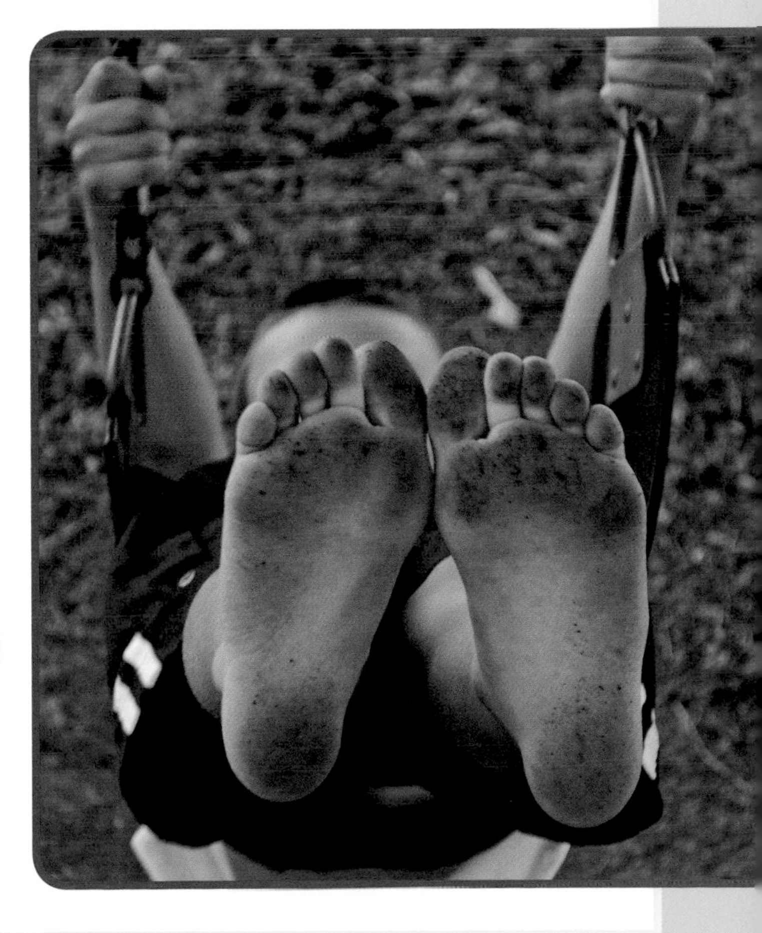

adaptation: The change a plant or animal goes through so that it is better able to live in a particular environment

atmosphere: The entire mass of air and gases that surround Earth

atmospheric pressure: The force applied in every direction by the atmosphere

barometer: An instrument that determines likely weather changes by measuring the changes in atmospheric pressure

bivalve: A type of mollusk that lives inside two connecting shells

chlorophyll: A green substance in plants that allows them to convert energy from the sun by photosynthesis

climate: Average weather conditions of a region

coastal area: The seashore or an area of land near the seashore

density: The amount of matter of a substance per unit of volume, or space, of the substance

depression: An area that is sunk below or lower than the surrounding areas

endangered species: Plants or animals that are in danger of no longer being found in the wild because of loss of habitat or threats from humans

exoskeleton: The outer supportive covering of an animal, such as on insects, spiders, or crustaceans

gastropod: A type of mollusk that has a muscular foot for moving, a distinct head, and commonly a spiral shell

glacier: A large, slow-moving mass of ice that forms over time from snow

Great Ice Age: A very long period of cold climate when glaciers covered large areas of land

habitat: Natural home of a plant or animal

illuminate: To provide light to something or light up

inhabitant: A person or animal that lives in a particular place or environment

interconnected: Applying to two or more things that are connected or related to each other

meteorologist: One who studies the science that deals with atmosphere and weather

migration: The regular movement of certain animals to and from an area, often connected to the change of seasons

mineral: A natural substance that is formed underground, such as diamond or salt

Northern Hemisphere: The half of Earth that exists north of the Equator

organism: Any individual living thing, such as a person, plant, or animal

paleontology: The science that deals with past living plants or animals through the recovery and study of fossils

pollination: The act of carrying the very fine dust produced by one plant to another, usually by insects or wind, so that the plant can produce seeds

refract: To cause a ray of light or energy to bend from a straight path when it passes through one medium to another, such as from air to water

sediment: The material deposited by water, wind, glaciers, or other factors that settles to the bottom of a liquid

suburb: A smaller community next to a city

temperate: Mild or moderate climate

tropical: The area on Earth between the Tropic of Cancer and the Tropic of Capricorn, where it is usually warm year-round

turbulence: Irregular, often up-and-down motions in the atmosphere

urban: Area where natural vegetation has been replaced by towns or cities

vegetation: The plant life covering an area

For resources that will help you plan your next outdoor adventure, check out these sites.

American Island Information
www.worldislandinfo.com/American%20Islands.html

America's State Parks
www.americasstateparks.org

Find a Local Playground: Kaboom
http://mapofplay.kaboom.org

Guide to Finding a Clean Beach
www.nrdc.org/water/oceans/ttw/guide.asp

National Geographic Kids Animals and Nature Stories
kids.nationalgeographic.com/kids/stories/animalsnature

National Park Foundation
www.nationalparks.org

National Wildlife Federation
www.nwf.org

Where to Go Forest Guide
www.discovertheforest.org/where-to-go

Illustrations are indicated by **boldface.** If illustrations are included within a page span, the entire span is **boldface.**

Captions for Chapter Opener Photos

12–13: A group of girls enjoy discovering creatures in a tide pool at the beach.
36–37: Leaping into the woods, this outdoor explorer is ready for some fun!
64–65: Hanging upside down from a tree is just one of the adventurous things you can do in the great outdoors!
90–91: Skaters glide across the ice surrounded by colorful fall foliage.
116–117: Riding a merry-go-round is the perfect way to spin into fun while at the park!

PHOTO CREDITS

IS: iStockphoto, SS: Shutterstock, GI: Getty Images, CO: Corbis, NGC: National Geographic Creative, NG: National Geographic

FRONT COVER: (Kid cartwheeling), plainpicture; (sand castle), Begsteiger/McPhoto/Capital Pictures; (kite), Vivian Fung/SS; (tree house), Don Klumpp/ Photographer's Choice/GI; (inner tube), Gary S Chapman/Photographer's Choice/GI; **BACK COVER:** Lori Epstein/NG; **FRONT MATTER:** 2-3, Peter Cade/Iconica/GI; 4 (UPLE), cappi thompson/SS; 4 (UPRT), Skip Brown/NGC; 4 (LO), Spyros Bourboulis/First Light/GI; 5 (UPLE), Lori Epstein/NG; 5 (UPRT), Orange-studio/SS; 5 (LO), Lori Epstein/NG; 6-7, Tracy van Eck/Urban Jungle Adventure Park; 8, swisshippo/IS; 9, bluehand/SS; **LET'S GET WET:** 12-13, Priscilla Gragg/Blend Images RM/GI; 14, Pierre Leclerc/SS; 15 (1), KonArt/IS; 15 (2), lena_volo/IS; 15 (3), Lindsay Douglas/SS; 15 (4), Colin Monteath/Minden Pictures; 15 (5), Peter Essick/NGC; 16-17, suprun/IS; 17 (UPLE), Dallas Stribley/Lonely Planet Images/GI; 17 (UPRT), Lisa Santore/IS; 17 (CTR), RainforestAustralia/IS; 17 (LOLE), DNY59/IS; 17 (LORT), Ken Wolter/IS; 18, Subbotina Anna/SS; 19 (UP), Lori Epstein/NGC; 19 (LOLE), Creative Crop/Digital Vision/GI; 19 (LORT), Will Selarep/IS; 20-21, Arterra Picture Library/ Alamy; 20 (A), David Hillerby/IS; 20 (B), AtWaG/IS; 21 (C), SuperStock; 21 (D), mrundbaken/IS; 21 (F), Lost Mountain Studio/SS; 21 (G), suemack/IS; 22-23, Seishi Nakano/Aflo/Score RF/GI; 22 (UP), Stephanie Rousseau/IS; 22 (LO), Doug Perrine/NPL/Minden Pictures; 23 (UP), Robert Koopmans/IS; 23 (LO), Joseph Gareri/IS; 24-25, kurdistan/SS; 25 (UP), Bob Gibbons/Alamy; 25 (CTR RT), FWStudio/SS; 25 (CTR LE), SOMMAI/SS; 25 (LOLE), Ammit Jack/SS; 25 (LORT), Elliotte Rusty Harold/ SS; 26-27, apsimo1/IS; 27 (B), Brendan Hunter/IS; 27 (C), Lars Johansson/IS; 27 (D), Nancy Nehring/IS; 27 (E), AtWaG/IS; 27 (F), Lee Rogers/IS; 28, Lori Epstein/NG; 29, Anna segeren/SS; 30-31, Patryk Kosmider/SS; 31 (UPLE), Rebell/IS; 31 (UPRT), Jim David/SS; 31 (LOLE), blackwaterimages/IS; 31 (LORT), Ruslan Dashinsky/IS; 32, Lori Epstein/NG; 33 (UP), pigphoto/IS; 33 (CTR LE), Sally Scott/SS; 33 (CTR RT), Feng Yu/SS; 33 (LO), Alexei Zaycev/IS; 34-35, cdascher/IS; 34 (A), Klaas Lingbeek-van Kranen/IS; 34 (B), 33karen33/IS; 35 (D), IS; 35 (E), Brian J. Skerry/NGC; 35 (F), Solvin Zankl/Visuals Unlimited/CO; 35 (G), G Tipene/SS; **JOURNEY THROUGH THE TREES:** 36-37, Walter Smith/Mint Images/the Agency Collection/GI; 38, Cultura RF/GI; 39 (1), SchmitzOlaf/IS; 39 (2), Sorin_Va/IS; 39 (3), seawhisper/SS; 39 (4), Dr. Gertrud Neumann-Denzau/NPL/Minden Pictures; 39 (5), blacksnapper/IS; 40-41, FooTToo/SS; 41 (UP), Rafal Dubiel/IS; 41 (CTR LE), sursad/ SS; 41 (CTR RT), Alan Jeffery/SS; 41 (LOLE), Alex ko/SS; 41 (LORT), Sergey Yechikov/SS; 42, Lori Epstein/NG; 43 (UPLE), Mirvav/SS; 43 (UPRT), Karen Zieff/Zieffphoto. com; 43 (LO), James Ac/SS; 44-45, mercedes rancaño/IS; 44 (B), Zoran Ivanovich/IS; 45 (C), Christine Glade/E+/GI; 45 (D), ArtTDi/SS; 45 (E), Vibe Images/SS; 45 (F), Stuart Monk/SS; 45 (G), Pamela N. Martin/Flickr RF/GI; 46 47, Dan Minicucci/NG Your Shot, 47 (UPLE), Norman Pogson/IS; 47 (UPRT), Mazdaguy03/IS; 47 (CTR), Sokolov Alexey/SS; 47 (LOLE), Svetlana Turilova/IS; 47 (LORT), LICreate/IS; 48-49, spxChrome/IS, 48 (UP), Jim Brandenburg/Minden Pictures; 48 (LO), Martin Ruegner/ Photodisc/GI; 49 (UP), Gerry Ellis/Minden Pictures; 49 (LO), Johner Images/Alamy; 50, Lori Epstein/NG; 51 (UP), Mantonature/IS; 51 (CTR), Lori Epstein/NG; 51 (LOLE), Lori Epstein/NG; 51 (LORT), The Bridgeman Art Library/GI; 52-53, Barbara Hesse/Visuals Unlimited/CO; 52 (B), pipedreams/IS; 53 (C), Stephan Pietzko/IS; 53 (D), Oliver Childs/IS; 53 (E), Chris and Tilde Stuart/FPLA/GI; 53 (F), Jack Dagley Photography/SS; 54-55, Lori Epstein/NG; 55 (UP), John Fedele/Blend Images/the Agency Collection/GI; 55 (LO), Lori Epstein/NG; 55, bogdan ionescu/SS; 56-57, keiichihiki/IS; 57 (UP), Frans Lanting Studio/Alamy; 57 (LOLE), BMJ/SS; 57 (LORT), Stephen Meese/IS; 58, Lori Epstein/NG; 59 (UP), Science Picture Co/Collection Mix: Subjects RM/GI; 59 (CTR), Lori Epstein/NG; 59 (LOLE), Garsya/IS; 59 (LORT), prudkov/IS; 60-61, L Lee Rue/FPLA/GI; 61 (B), Matt Jeppson/SS; 61 (C), danz13/SS; 61 (D), Sebastian Kennerknecht/Minden Pictures; 61 (E), ColbyJoe/IS; 61 (F), imagebroke/ Alamy; 62 (UP), courtesy Buuveibaatar Bayarbaatar; 62 (LO), courtesy Dana Bunnell-Young; 63 (UP), courtesy Mariana Fuentes; 63 (CTR), courtesy Rob Parsons/ Mariana Fuentes; 63 (LO), courtesy Isabelle Charrier; **EXPLORE YOUR BACKYARD:** 64-65, John Nordell/Photolibrary RM/GI; 66-67, Raymond Forbes/SuperStock; 67 (1), John T. Schneider/TheGardenMaze.com; 67 (2), GarysFRP/IS; 67 (3), Dennis Barnes/Britain on View RM/GI; 67 (4), Moments by Mullineux/SS; 67 (5), Brooks Kraft/CO; 68-69, jodi jacobson/IS; 69 (UPLE), Visuals Unlimited/GI; 69 (UPRT), Oktay Ortakcioglu/IS; 69 (LOLE), Frank Leung/IS; 69 (LORT), johnandersonphoto/IS; 70-71, Lori Epstein/NG; 71, NASA (UP); 71, ajbarr/IS (LO); 72-73, gordondix/IS; 72 (A), isak55/SS; 72 (B), SS; 73 (C), Volkova Anna/SS; 73 (D), danmitchell/IS; 73 (E), Volkova Anna/SS; 73 (F), SS; 73 (G), th3fisa/SS; 74-75, Viorika/IS; 74 (UP), pollypic/IS; 74 (LO), Alexander Kurlovich/Alamy; 75 (UP), Michael Guttman/IS; 75 (LO), R Speckart/SS; 76-77, pastorscott/IS; 77 (UPLE), Videowokart/SS: 77 (UPRT), javarman/SS; 77 (CTR), Steve Byland/IS; 77 (LOLE), Matt Jeppson/SS; 77 (LORT), pzig98/ SS; 78, Ron Hilton/SS, 79 (UP), cjlws/SS; 79 (LO), Margaret M Stewart/SS; 80-81, haoliang/IS; 80 (B), Chris Humphries/SS; 81 (C), MBurnham/IS; 81 (D), Lynn_Bystrom/IS; 81 (E), Jason Mintzer/SS; 81 (F), Rob Hainer/SS; 81 (G), oddrose/IS; 82, Richard Loader/IS; 83 (LO), small_frog/IS; 83 (UP), Rolf Nussbaumer Photography/Alamy; 83 (CTR), Carlos Mora/Alamy; 83 (LO), Andy Hallam/Alamy; 84-85, Hill Street Studios/Blend Images/GI; 85 (UP), Nancy Nehring/IS; 85 (CTR), Joyce Johnsen/IS; 85 (LOLE), Pacific Northwest Photo/SS; 85 (LORT), Pi-Lens/SS; 86-87, Lori Epstein/NG; 87 (UP), O. Louis Mazzatenta/NGC; 87 (LOLE), songphon/IS; 87 (LORT), INTERFOTO/Alamy; 88-89, Geoffrey Kuchera/IS; 88 (B), Mastering_Microstock/SS; 89 (C), Steve Byland/SS; 89 (D), Mark Herreid/SS; 89 (E), Martin Fowler/ SS; 89 (F), Roberto Cerruti/SS; **NATURE AROUND TOWN:** 90-91, Mitchell Funk/Photographer's Choice/GI; 92-93, YinYang/IS; 93 (1), Tracy van Eck/Urban Jungle Adventure Park; 93 (2), Joe Potato Photo/IS; 93 (3), Ferran Traité Soler/IS; 93 (4), euroluftbildde/SuperStock; 93 (5), SeanPavonePhoto/SS; 94-95, paul mansfield photography/Flickr RF/GI; 95 (UP), DyMax/SS; 95 (LO), tpnagasima/IS; 96, Lori Epstein/NG; 97 (UP), MustafaNC/SS; 97 (CTR), Jane Rix/SS; 97 (LO), Anthony Rosenberg/IS; 98-99, lucato/IS; 98 (B), Tim Laman/NGC; 98 (C), Palmer Kane LLC/SS; 99 (D), StoryTeller/IS; 99 (E), Tom Reichner/SS; 99 (F), Igor Chekalin/SS; 99 (G), Olivier Lantzendörffer/IS; 100-101, Rachel Lewis/Lonely Planet Images/GI; 100 (UP), Lori Epstein/NGC; 100 (LO), Bill Hebel/AIA; 101 (UP), Eric Brown/Alamy; 101 (LO), Sam Harrel/News-Miner/Fairbanks Daily News-Miner/ZUMAPRESS/Alamy; 102-103, kali9/E+/GI; 103 (UP), Scott Leman/SS; 103 (LOLE), iNoppadol/SS; 103 (LORT), Eric Isselée/IS; 104, Lori Epstein/NG; 105 (UP), Villamilk/IS; 105 (CTR LE), Lori Epstein/NG; 105 (CTR RT), Lori Epstein/NG; 105 (LO), Sever180/SS; 105, GrigoryL/SS; 106-107, Lisa Thornberg/IS; 106 (B), Alex Wild/Visuals Unlimited/CO; 107 (C), anat chant/SS; 107 (D), Suede Chen/SS; 107 (E), Muellek Josef/SS; 107 (F), Spanishalex/IS; 107 (G), Brandon Alms/SS; 108-109, Dave Bevan/Alamy; 109 (UP), Karen Faljyan/SS; 109 (LO), Eugene Bochkarev/IS; 110-111, Thinkstock/Comstock Images/GI; 111 (UPLE), Frank Hildebrand/IS; 111 (UPRT), Eldad Carin/SS; 111 (LOLE), SPrada/IS; 111 (LORT), Lori Epstein/NG; 112-113, Lori Epstein/NG; 113 (UP), Konrad Wothe/Minden Pictures; 113 (CTR), Lori Epstein/NG; 113 (LO), DeAgostini/GI; 114-115, Jeff Goulden/IS; 114 (B), Hans Neleman/Photodisc/GI; 115 (C), Dirk Wiersma/Science Source; 115 (D), Alexander Bark/SS; 115 (E), Pete Ryan/NG RF/GI; 115 (F), Giovanni Rinaldi/IS; 115 (G), Dr Ajay Kumar Singh/SS; **LET'S GO TO THE PARK:** 116-117, Renee Keith/E+/GI; 118, Chris Schwalm; 119 (1), JeniFoto/SS; 119 (2), EcoPrint/SS; 119 (3), moizhusein/SS; 119 (4), michieldb/IS; 119 (5), Christopher Meder/SS; 120-121, kavram/IS; 121 (UP), Takeshi.K/Flickr RF/GI; 121 (CTR LE), Paul Giamou/IS; 121 (CTR RT), William P Howell/IS; 121 (LO), espiegle/IS; 122-123, Lori Epstein/NG; 123 (UP), Georgios Kollidas/SS; 123 (LOLE), Lori Epstein/NG; 123 (LOCTR), Lori Epstein/NG; 123 (LORT), Lori Epstein/NG; 124-125, kredo/ SS; 124 (B), Mona Makela/SS; 124 (C), ivy photo/SS; 125 (D), ANATOL/SS; 125 (E), Oleksii Sagitov/SS; 125 (F), Tamara Kulikova/SS; 125 (LORT), David Aguilar; 126-127, sburel/IS; 126 (UP), RiverNorthPhotography/IS; 126 (LO), Tom Bean/Alamy; 127 (UP), James Randklev/SuperStock; 127 (LO), Christian Kober/GI; 128-129, Marina Degtyareva/IS; 129 (UP), Clint Farlinger/Alamy; 129 (CTR), Tom Reichner/SS; 129 (LO), AP Images/George Ruhe; 130, Lori Epstein/NG; 131 (UP), Malcolm Schuyl/Alamy; 131 (LO), Lori Epstein/NG; 132-133, Gennady/IS; 132 (B), René Mansi/IS; 133 (C), Somogyvari/IS; 133 (D), freerangestock/IS; 133 (E), leezsnow/IS; 133 (F), Maridav/SS; 133 (RT), Creativeye99/IS; 134, Lori Epstein/NG; 135 (1), Lori Epstein/NG; 135 (3), Lori Epstein/NG; 135 (4), Lori Epstein/NG; 135 (5), Lori Epstein/NG; 136-137, Eduardo Jose Bernardino/IS; 137 (UP), SuperStock; 137 (LOLE), irin-k/SS; 137 (LO CTR), Serge Bertasius/IS; 137 (LORT), shorrocks/IS; 138-139, Lori Epstein/ NG; 139 (1), Lori Epstein/NG; 139 (2), Lori Epstein/NG; 139 (3), Lori Epstein/NG; 139 (LO), Chris Clinton/IS; 140-141, Erik Bettini/IS; 140 (B), Paul Reeves Photography/ SS; 141 (C), Frank Leung/IS; 141 (D), Martha Marks/SS; 141 (E), Feng Yu/SS; 141 (F), Dennis Donohue/SS; 141 (G), Tom Reichner/SS; 141 (RT), NaturesDisplay/IS; 142 (UP), courtesy Mbunya Francis Nkemnyi; 142 (LO), courtesy Stephen Sillett; 143 (UP), courtesy Becca Skinner; 143 (LO), courtesy Tshewang Wangchuk; **BACK MATTER:** 144-145, David Roth/Taxi/GI; 146 (inset), Charles Dharapak/AFP/GI; 146-147, Mark Wilson/GI; 153, Colleen Rudolph/Flickr/GI

National Geographic gratefully acknowledges Richard Louv for his inspiration, expertise, and guidance with this book.

To my parents, who always encouraged me to drop the remote control and get outside—N. H.

Special thanks to Denise Howe at Mary Collins School at Cherry Valley—J. B.

Published by the National Geographic Society
John M. Fahey, *Chairman of the Board and Chief Executive Officer*
Declan Moore, *Executive Vice President; President, Publishing and Travel*
Melina Gerosa Bellows, *Publisher; Chief Creative Officer, Books, Kids, and Family*

Prepared by the Book Division
Hector Sierra, *Senior Vice President and General Manager*
Nancy Laties Feresten, *Senior Vice President, Kids Publishing and Media*
Jennifer Emmett, *Vice President, Editorial Director, Kids Books*
Eva Absher-Schantz, *Design Director, Kids Publishing and Media*
Jay Sumner, *Director of Photography, Kids Publishing*
R. Gary Colbert, *Production Director*
Jennifer A. Thornton, *Director of Managing Editorial*

Staff for This Book
Priyanka Lamichhane, *Project Editor*
Jim Hiscott, Jr., *Art Director*
Lori Epstein, *Senior Photo Editor*
Project Design Company, *Designer*
Stuart Armstrong, *Graphics Artist*
Carl Mehler, *Director of Maps*
Ariane Szu-Tu, *Editorial Assistant*
Paige Towler, Editorial Intern
Callie Broaddus, *Design Production Assistant*
Margaret Leist, *Photo Assistant*
Grace Hill, *Associate Managing Editor*
Michael O'Connor, *Production Editor*
Lewis R. Bassford, *Production Manager*
Susan Borke, *Legal and Business Affairs*

Production Services
Phillip L. Schlosser, *Senior Vice President*
Chris Brown, *Vice President, NG Book Manufacturing*
George Bounelis, *Senior Production Manager*
Nicole Elliott, *Director of Production*
Rachel Faulise, *Manager*
Robert L. Barr, *Manager*

The National Geographic Society is one of the world's largest nonprofit scientific and educational organizations. Founded in 1888 to "increase and diffuse geographic knowledge," the Society's mission is to inspire people to care about the planet. It reaches more than 400 million people worldwide each month through its official journal, *National Geographic*, and other magazines; National Geographic Channel; television documentaries; music; radio; films; books; DVDs; maps; exhibitions; live events; school publishing programs; interactive media; and merchandise. National Geographic has funded more than 10,000 scientific research, conservation and exploration projects and supports an education program promoting geographic literacy.

For more information, please visit nationalgeographic.com, call 1-800-NGS LINE (647-5463), or write to the following address:
National Geographic Society
1145 17th Street N.W.
Washington, D.C. 20036-4688 U.S.A.

Visit us online at nationalgeographic.com/books

For librarians and teachers: ngchildrensbooks.org

More for kids from National Geographic: kids.nationalgeographic.com

For information about special discounts for bulk purchases, please contact National Geographic Books Special Sales: ngspecsales@ngs.org

For rights or permissions inquiries, please contact National Geographic Books Subsidiary Rights: ngbookrights@ngs.org

Trade paperback ISBN: 978-1-4263-1502-2
Reinforced library edition ISBN: 978-1-4263-1503-9

Printed in the United States of America
14/QGT-CML/1